THE SUCCESSFUL SPEAKER

273 TIPS FOR
POWERFUL PRESENTATIONS

Ashwood
House

To order further copies of this book or to contact the author,
please visit our website at **Ashwood-House.com**

orders@ashwood-house.com

There is a website which accompanies this book. Please visit
http://www.Speaker-Tips.com
for online resources, links and latest updates.

© 2007 Dr Mandar Marathe
http://www.Mandar-Marathe.com

Published by Ashwood House Publishing
7 Durham Way, Parkgate, Rotherham S62 6FL, UK
+44 1709 528 528

info@ashwood-house.com
http://www.Ashwood-House.com

British Library Cataloguing-in-Publication Data
A catalogue record for this book is available from the British Library

ISBN-10: 0-9554873-0-7
ISBN-13: 978-0-9554873-0-9

THE SUCCESSFUL SPEAKER

273 TIPS FOR
POWERFUL PRESENTATIONS

DR MANDAR MARATHE

"The only reason to give a speech is to change the world"
– John F. Kennedy (1917–1963), 35th President of the USA

Ashwood House

Dedicated to Mr M. Y. & Dr (Mrs) M. M. Mahajan:
– My grandparents, who inspired me to write books

Brief Contents

Detailed Contents

Introduction

Congratulations! You have just received an invitation to talk at an international conference next month at an exotic foreign destination.

Or maybe you've been asked to present your research data at an inter-departmental scientific meeting. Did you say you have to present a business case for your "once-in-a-lifetime opportunity" to your CEO?

This is fantastic news – you should be really excited!

Although you might be dreading the idea right now (you may well be tempted to simply decline the invitation politely), I don't think you should be quite so hasty.

➤ Whatever the scenario, the bottom line is that you have to stand up in front of a group of people, and perform some public speaking.

Does that idea fill you with dread? I know exactly what you're going through.

In fact, most people experience some nervousness before giving a presentation. You can't mistake the symptoms: a dry mouth, palpitations, sweaty palms, and a sense of impending doom and destruction! Upto a third of people admit that this fear is a big problem in their professional lives, and some studies have shown that one in every twenty people suffers so badly that it might actually be affecting their career progression.

My own story

I can remember being absolutely petrified of public speaking tasks during English lessons as a shy teenager at school. I was always the last one to "volunteer" to read aloud a passage from a book or give a speech.

When I left school at 18 and went to university to study medicine I thought that would be the end of public speaking for ever. Can you imagine my horror when I found out that as a medical student too I would be required to give talks and presentations?

One particular presentation stands out in my mind. In December 1995 I was half way through medical school. We were each required to select, research and present the case of an interesting patient that we had seen, to an audience of 30 of my fellow students and our tutors at one of our weekly seminars.

Naturally, I was in denial about this approaching event for several weeks. I stupidly kept putting off the preparation until it was almost too late. And then I found myself panicking and desperately struggling to meet the deadline.

After a few days and nights surviving on black coffee and chocolate, the day of the presentation finally dawned. At 6am I collapsed on my bed in a cold sweat, feeling sick, dizzy and having a racing heart. I somehow managed to calm down and carried myself and my OHP transparencies to the seminar room.

The actual talk itself is now a blur. I remember standing up in front of the class and fumbling through the sheets of papers on which I had scribbled my entire script. My voice was feeble and croaky. My mouth was dry and I could hardly get the words out. I was covered in sweat. Yes folks, I was a complete nervous wreck and everyone who was there in the room that day knew about it. Boy was that embarrassing...!

At the end of the talk I was completely drained, and went home and just slept for several days to recover.

A turning point (my light bulb moment)

All in all, that day was a remarkably traumatic experience. But it was a turning point in my life because it made me face up to some realities.

>   1) **I realised that I could not carry on like that**: I did not want to experience such a terrible event ever again. I was not strong enough to go through this on a regular basis.

>   2) Equally, I accepted that I would have to give presentations and talks for the rest of my working life. Until that point I was in denial, and thought I could escape from public speaking – maybe I could find a career where I would not be required to talk in public. However, it was now time to finally accept defeat: **this escapist strategy was simply not going to work**.

>   3) I also accepted a fact that is now so obvious. That my nerves, anxiety and fears were ruining my performance. I did not prepare in time because I hated the very suggestion of standing up in front of an audience; I could not perform to the best of my potential as I was so nervous. **The barrier to my success was within myself**. I realised that if I could eliminate my negativity, there was a real chance that I could do a reasonable presentation.

>   4) I could see people around me who were getting praised for giving better presentations than mine. Yet they had put in fewer hours than I had, stressed and struggled less than I had, and drank less coffee than I had! Yes, **I was envious of other people's success**.

So that day I made a personal resolution. I promised never to put myself through such an ordeal again. I decided to sit down and brainstorm about how I could give better presentations.

I started to examine people who gave good lectures and presentations, and analyse their style and techniques. I also examined those who were poor at public speaking to see what mistakes they made. I made a resolution to learn from my own mistakes and make a conscious effort to overcome my nerves. I would practice as much as possible, and actively get feedback.

I was realistic about my aims: I did not expect to ever become a "smooth talker", but I hoped that eventually I could at least become comfortable with public speaking. By hook or by crook I would have to learn the skill of public speaking.

Light at the end of the tunnel

Since that fateful day in 1995, have collected, from a wide range of sources, a whole wealth of experience, advice, hints and tips on how to give a powerful, successful talk or presentation.

➤ This book is a synthesis of that body of wisdom.

Since that day, I have presented at a range of talks, tutorials, departmental meetings, seminars, international conferences, etc. and have achieved a level of competence such that I no longer dread being asked to speak in public.

This journey of discovery and development has taken me more than 10 years. That truly disappoints me, as I don't think it should necessarily take 10 years to acquire these skills, attitudes and experience.

My motivation in writing this book is to condense the necessary information into a readily-accessible, digestible and practical format, so that you, the reader, will not have to spend 10 years struggling as I did.

So with this sincere intention in mind, I now present to you my collection of 273 tips to delivering a powerful presentation so that you can become the successful speaker that you deserve to be.

About the author

Dr Mandar Marathe graduated from Southampton University with an honours degree in Biomedical Sciences in 1998 and a Bachelor of Medicine degree in 1999. He holds advanced qualifications in Emergency Medicine and in Toxicology.

He juggles a career as a doctor working in Accident & Emergency, while raising three children with his wife, writing books, and endlessly surfing the internet looking for the next "big thing".

With almost two decades of public speaking experience in both academic and professional arenas, he is today an enthusiastic and popular educator who is well qualified to share his ideas about what makes a successful speaker and a powerful presentation.

How to use this book

This book contains a range of tips which can help you improve the way you give oral presentations in business or academia.

> This book does not contain **all** the answers.

Rather, it is intended as an aid to reflection and inspiration – a resource that you can draw upon in preparation for your presentation.

You may use this book as a complete blueprint for giving a presentation, if you so wish. However, I would recommend that a more productive approach would be to take the tips and concepts presented here and mix them with your own personality, creativity and style, with due consideration to your own time constraints and "comfort zone", to generate unique and personalised ideas on how you can improve your presentations.

This book is designed to offer you maximum flexibility in terms of how you use it.

1) You can sit down for a couple of hours and read it **cover to cover**. This is the recommended way, especially for beginners or those who want to gain the full benefit from a book like this.

   A word of caution though – this book is the result of over 10 years of study and experience. It would be easy to feel overwhelmed by the amount of information you find here. Once you have read the whole book, I suggest you then identify particular sections or tips that interest you and work on more manageable chunks of the book at a time.

2) You can follow the chapters and sections from start to finish and use them as a **checklist** or **timeline** for preparing your next presentation.

3) You can select one **chapter** or **section** at a time, and work to incorporate the ideas you find into your own presentation style.

4) You can look at the **Table of Contents** and jump straight to the tips that particularly interest you.

The book has generous margins to enable you to annotate the text with your own interpretations, personal notes, ideas and thoughts.

Each tip is graded as being one of "Essential", "Intermediate" or "Advanced". This grading system allows you to tailor your use of the book to your own level of experience and confidence. There is something of benefit for everyone, irrespective of your current level of skill in public speaking.

You will read some of the tips and feel that the ideals they portray are too lofty, unrealistic or unachievable. I make no apology: this has been done intentionally to inspire and motivate the reader to strive, to stretch, to reach for an ideal which may or may not be immediately attainable.

You will also find some contradictory advice in different parts of the book! This is because there is no single, universal "right answer" – you must find what is right for you, your objective and your audience's needs.

The book is deliberately written in a very practical style; a large amount of sound educational theory underpins much of the advice in this book, but this has been excluded in the interests of clarity and to maintain a practical focus. There are many books on the market which cover these theoretical aspects.

http://www.Speaker–Tips.com

This website accompanies the book. You will find further resources, links, and examples related to many of the themes you will find inside the book.

If you wish to offer suggestions for improvements to the book, please contact me through the email contact form on the website.

Who needs this book?

For the sake of consistency, the term "presentation" is used throughout the book.

In reality, your presentation can be anything which involves talking in front of other people, whether it is:

- ✓ A lecture
- ✓ A speech
- ✓ A business proposal
- ✓ A report
- ✓ A talk
- ✓ A project report
- ✓ A conference presentation

- ✓ A keynote speech
- ✓ An after-dinner speech
- ✓ A presentation in a seminar
- ✓ Teaching students
- ✓ Presenting research results
- ✓ Talking to the press
- ✓ Presenting ideas in business settings

Anyone who is engaged in these activities will find a wealth of ideas and tips in this book, no matter what their level of skill or expertise is.

"There are three cardinal rules of public speaking: 1) Speak about something you have earned the right to talk about through experience or study, 2) Be excited about your subject, 3) Be eager to share your talk with your listeners."
– Dale Carnegie (1888-1955), American writer

Chapter 1: Planning for your presentation

Tip 1: Respect the process of preparing for a presentation	Essential

We need to get some things straight, before we start preparing for your presentation.

The preparation for your presentation starts right here with Tip Number 1 – with you mentally accepting and believing that the preparation for your presentation is at least as important as – if not more important than – your delivery on the day of the presentation itself.

You may be a born natural public speaker with the most confident and comfortable style of talking. But unless you have done your preparation, you won't be able to achieve anything worthwhile with your skills.

I am sure you have at times sat in an audience and watched a well-polished professional speaker delivering a fact-filled, smoothly flowing seminar, making the business of speaking look easy. But before even professional speakers can succeed at their trade, they must also perfect their speaking skills.

Great speakers constantly work on ways to improve their performances. They continually hire speech and drama coaches. They spend their free time researching new materials and in rehearsals. They accumulate and learn from a vast amount of practical experience.

But do not be fooled. While there may be 0.1% who are "naturals", for the rest of us it takes a great deal of preparation and hard work to achieve this natural look. It is because of this preparation that some speakers are good, not despite it.

It does take a surprisingly long time to prepare for a good presentation, and a lot of work goes into it – the vast majority of this human investment is not seen by the general public audience.

➢ **There are no shortcuts: Preparation is the key to a successful talk.**

So get yourself psyched-up for it *now*. I don't want you to be one of those fools (like I have been in the past) who procrastinate and delay their preparation. Maybe they don't realise the importance of preparation or maybe they are simply running scared. Or maybe they are arrogant enough to think they can pull off a great presentation without any preparation?

Let me give you some figures...

If you know the material well...
...it is reasonable to spend 10 hours
in preparation for each hour of presentation

If you don't know the material well or if you find the material challenging...
...it is reasonable to spend 20 hours
in preparation for each hour of presentation

*If you don't know the material well or if you find the material challenging
but you still want to give a great presentation...*
...it is reasonable to spend 30 hours
in preparation for each hour of presentation

I think you get the point.

➢ So go right now and clear out some time in your diary!

Yes, cancel some commitments. You can go to the cinema *after* your presentation is out of the way. You can spend time with the kids after the presentation is over. If this presentation is important to you then make that sacrifice. You won't regret it.

Tip 2: Avoid avoidance	Essential

In my experience, people who are worried about giving a presentation tend to put off thinking about it and they delay preparing for it until the last minute. Ironically, this makes their situation worse because on top of dealing with their anxiety they also have to contend with time pressures.

All too often the result is a hurriedly put together set of disjointed slides and a presentation which is an embarrassment for both the presenter and the audience.

➢ It doesn't have to be like this!

One favour you can do for yourself is this: don't make your burden greater than it already is, by leaving your presentation to the last minute. Allow yourself plenty to time – as much as you feasibly can – to prepare for your presentation. I am sure you will thank me for this tip later on.

Tip 3: Tackle the root cause of your fear	Essential

When the mere thought of giving a presentation brings you out in a cold sweat and makes you bury your head under your pillow, you can take comfort in the fact that at least you are not alone! Most people have a fear of giving presentations. This is normal. It is a form of panic which is very similar to the "stage fright" that most actors experience.

If you are scared of public speaking, it can be helpful for you to consider where exactly the fear comes from. If you can identify what it is about public speaking that makes you panic, you can then figure out how to tackle it.

Introverts

For some people it's a fear of feeling exposed in front of strangers. A fear of feeling "naked" in public. Typically introverts would prefer to stay at home, or at least, hide behind the lectern and a pile of written notes. Such shy types may wow the audience with very complicated slides in an attempt to divert all the attention away from themselves.

If this describes you, then you have my sympathy because I personally can strongly relate with you. It is futile to try to change this aspect of your personality because such traits are deeply wired in.

What may be much more effective is for you to identify a positive role model and develop a "public persona" – call it a mask if you want – that you can put on and off whenever you like. There is no need to show the public your inner private soul – why should you? But for the purpose of your presentation, go ahead and invent a new dimension to your personality which you can use to face the public with.

Fear of embarrassment

Many people experience a fear of public speaking which can be traced to a fear of the audience finding out their weakness, flaws and insecurities. Normal, otherwise happy, confident and strong personalities can be reduced to sweating, trembling wrecks because of an irrational feeling that the audience will find out, once and for all, that they are not as smart or cool or "in control" as they had previously been led to believe.

The solution to this problem is similar to the advice I give to introverts – you must build a strong wall around yourself and project a robust image that you are happy for people to see. A useful way to do this is to practice public speaking with your new persona as much as possible and whenever you can.

Fear of failure / fear of the consequences of failure

Lets be frank – developing solid skills in public speaking are paramount to climbing the career ladder in many professions. Those who do not master the necessary skills in an appropriate time-frame will be left behind by those who can.

Naturally, when it comes to giving a presentation, people do realise that a lot may be riding on this event. That pressure damages performance.

The good news is that if you follow the tips in this book, you will have significantly and dramatically reduced your chances of failure. I hope you take some comfort from that fact.

And even if you do fail – you can take solace in the fact that even professional speakers sometimes fail because they did not research adequately, or because the audience was hostile, for example. In such situations you just have to pick yourself up and move on.

You must analyse your own personality and see what is making you put up this barrier to success. And that's exactly what it is - an unnecessary barrier to you achieving your goals. Fortunately, it is a problem that you can solve.

You must learn to channel your energy into something constructive and positive – such as doing *more* research, spending *more* time practicing, making *doubly* sure you reach the venue on time, and making sure you apply as many of the tips from this book as you can.

Tip 4: Make sure the topic is right for you	Essential

Before you truly launch into the planning of your presentation, step back and think about whether this is the right presentation for you to be doing. Is it the right topic for you, and are you the right person for this topic? Rather than the person who invited you, you yourself should know whether it is appropriate for you to be giving this presentation.

Maybe you have been given the freedom to select a topic of your choice, in which case you are clearly onto a winner! You simply can't go wrong. Just skip over this tip and read on for advice about how to select the right topic.

If you are not so lucky and have been given a pre-set title or subject area, then think carefully about whether you can do it justice. Be sincere about this though, and never decline an invitation simply out of fear of public speaking.

"I already know about this topic"

If you are the resident expert on this topic, then jump into it head-first because having expertise and enthusiasm are key ingredients for a successful presentation.

A word of caution though – remember to take into consideration the level of expertise of your audience in relation to your own.

"I could do some research into this topic"

Think about your own level of expertise right now, and whether it will be possible to research the topic further. Think about how much time is required to gather data, whether you have the tools to analyse, process and comprehend the information, and the likely learning needs of your audience.

If you feel it would be possible to get up to speed on the given topic in a timely fashion, then carry on and commit yourself to doing just that.

If you are a student, remember that students are often deliberately given topics that they know nothing about – the research for the presentation is part of the learning process.

"I don't know about this topic, and I cannot research it"

If because of time pressures or your complete lack of interest in the field, you feel that you are not able to give the audience what they may want from this presentation, then it is best to politely decline the invitation as soon as possible. It is common courtesy to recommend someone else may be able to do it, if possible.

Generally, you should decline an invitation if you are not sufficiently knowledgeable on the topic and are not able to prepare for it, if you feel you are not the right person for the job, or if you think that you cannot give the audience what they need.

Tip 5: Make your speech great	Essential

Demosthenes, the father of Greek oratory, described four elements of a great speech:

- A great person
- A great occasion
- A great message
- A great delivery

You might not always be that great **person** giving a speech on a great **occasion** with a great **message** and great **delivery**. However, there are nonetheless, things you can do to improve in your favour the odds of giving a great speech.

Be a great person

Become a great person in the eyes of the audience, and be the best person that you can be. Let your experience, values, character, vision, even your sense of humour permeate every word you say and how you say it. Do the best research and preparation you can. Let yourself shine through in what you say.

Make it a great occasion

Think of any occasion that you speak as being a great occasion for you. Make it memorable and useful, so that your audience will look back and think of it also as being a great occasion because of you and your presentation.

Have a great message

Creating a memorable message takes preparation. Develop one idea that you truly care about and that the audience will benefit from. Be as clear and honest as you can be. Don't try to impress the audience. Care about your audience and for your message and convey your message with sincerity.

Give a great delivery

The only sure way to improve delivery is to practice. Know what you want to say and how you plan on saying it. Don't memorize your speech word for word. Establish eye contact, one person at a time. Speak from the heart, with passion.

As you prepare for your presentation, always be thinking about how you can be a **greater** person, how to make it a **greater** occasion, how to make it a **greater** message, and how to give a **greater** delivery.

Part A: Contact the event organiser

As soon as you have decided to go ahead with the presentation, you should contact the event organiser to confirm your acceptance of the invitation, and to clarify some of the organisational details surrounding your presentation.

Tip 6: Ask for a smaller room	Intermediate

If you have a choice, ask the organiser of your event to give you the smallest room possible for your presentation. A packed room is a more emotional room. It makes for better acoustics and eye contact.

If you have a small number of people in a large room, the tendency is often for some people to sit at the back and disengage with the speaker or the rest of the audience. This makes your task a lot harder – you will have to shout louder and it is more difficult to pick up on their non-verbal cues. In the worst case, they may start talking amongst themselves and you will struggle to regain control of the environment.

It is better to have 210 people crammed into a 200-person room than to have the same 200 people spread out in a 500-person room. You want people to say about your presentation, "it was standing room only."

Tip 7: Find out what technology is available	Essential

Well in advance of your event, talk with the person who is responsible for providing the technology for your presentation, whether it is a 35mm slide projector, overhead projector or a computer and projector combination.

This person may be the event organiser, or in large purpose-built venues such as conference centres there may be a team of technical support staff who are responsible for managing these facilities.

You should also find out which (1) operating system version and (2) presentation software version is running on the machine you will be using. If you have to save your presentation slide set down to an older software version you must check the slides before your presentation because slide formatting, transition and animation settings can be rendered differently between different versions of the same software product.

Remember that older computers may have CD readers only and may not be able to read your slide files at all if you burnt the slide set onto DVD from your more modern computer.

If you have a laptop computer, give consideration to the option of taking it with you and running your slides from your own laptop. If you decide to do this, you should nonetheless have contingency plans in case of computer failure.

Tip 8: Choose the timing of your presentation	Intermediate

Sometimes you will have no control over the timing of your presentation. However, if you are given the option, ask to speak at a time when the audience will be fresh. They will be more apt to listen to you, follow along with your stories, appreciate your humour, and engage with your presentation. This receptive time is generally at the beginning of an event, or in the morning.

Avoid speaking in the afternoon when the audience will have had lunch and will be naturally sleepy. It is more difficult to engage with such an audience. It is difficult enough to give a great presentation – why increase the challenge by having to lift the audience out of the doldrums?

At events such as conferences which may be held over several days, try to speak on the first day when delegates are naturally fresh, enthusiastic and excited. Avoid speaking in the afternoon of the last day when the audience is tired and everyone is thinking about the journey home!

Finally, if you know there will be a speaker who is extremely prominent or popular, it is best to avoid speaking *immediately before* that speaker as people will be eager for your presentation to finish. Likewise, avoid speaking *immediately after* that speaker as it may be difficult to follow in his or her wake.

Tip 9: Liaise with other speakers	Advanced

You should aim to give your audience a unique, personalised presentation (*see also "Tip 114: Personalise the slides for each audience", page 63*). A useful way to do this is to make your presentation link in with those of other people who are presenting on the same day or at the same event. You can illustrate how your ideas or data relate with those of the other presenters and the value and uniqueness of everyone's presentations will increase.

It helps to know as early as possible who else will be presenting, to give you sufficient time to plan how your presentation will be affected by those of the other people. Get in touch with the organiser of the event right now and find out with whom you are sharing a stage.

Tip 10: Confirm the date, time and venue	Essential

Check with the organiser as to the date, time and venue of your presentation. Plan your journey well in advance. Make sure you get maps, directions, parking information and hotel bookings organised in good time.

Part B: Do some research

You need to do a good amount of background research and fact-finding before you start making your slides or OHP transparencies.

Tip 11: Find out about your audience	Essential

If you already know exactly who your audience will be, then you can probably skip over this tip. If you are presenting to people who you already know, then you have an enormous advantage over someone who is going to face an audience they have never previously met.

Your aim in giving this presentation is to give your audience:

- **Something that they want**
  (See: "Tip 12: Give your audience what they want", page 15)

- **Something that is important for them**
  (See: "Tip 13: Have something important to say", page 16)

- **Something that is interesting to them**
  (See: "Tip 14: Have something interesting to say", page 16)

- **Something that is relevant to them**
  (See: "Tip 15: Have something relevant to say", page 16)

Clearly you cannot even hope to achieve these aims unless you have a good idea of who your audience is.

So before you begin to formulate the content of your presentation, make detailed enquiries into the makeup of your audience. You need to know who they are, why they are listening to your presentation, what their previous knowledge of the topic is, what they intend to do with the ideas you will convey through your presentation, and what their expectations of you are.

You need to know whether they are experts in the field, how much knowledge and jargon you can take for granted and how much background you will have to explain. You would feel better armed if you knew precisely what their opinions, prejudices, preconceived notions and agendas were.

You may also want to know whether the members of your audience already know each other, or whether they will be strangers amongst themselves. Also vitally important is an in-depth knowledge of their cultural and ethnic background, their likes and their dislikes.

You will only be able to give your audience something interesting, important, relevant and something that they want if you know them very well. You need this information in order to become the best possible presenter for that particular audience.

Tip 12: Give your audience what they want	Essential

A fundamental premise of marketing science is that a business should produce and sell things which customers are likely to want. If a business produced and sold items which customers simply did not want, that enterprise would soon be out of business!

A similar principle applies when you are giving your presentation. You must identify what your customers (audience) *want* from you, and then endeavour to fulfil that desire. If you fail to identify exactly what your customers (audience) want from you, then you will find yourself struggling to connect or engage with them.

I would take this principle one step further by saying that you should give your audience not only something that they want, but that you should give them something that they *need*.

Every presentation is about meeting your audience's needs. So when you are planning your presentation, do not focus on what interests you about your subject, or why you think your audience *should* be interested in what you have to say. Instead concentrate on your audience's point of view and how your idea or argument could and will benefit them.

Tip 13: Have something important to say	Essential

When you are planning your presentation, imagine yourself standing up in front of your expectant audience at the start of your presentation, looking each person in the eye and telling them, "What I am about to tell you now is the most important thing you will hear today..."

You should aim to tell your audience something important. In fact, you should yourself believe that what you want to tell them is the most important thing in the world. OK, maybe that's an exaggeration, but at least you should be satisfied that what you are going to tell them is something of significance and that when they have heard what you have to say, their lives will be changed because of it.

If you cannot, hand on heart, believe that yourself about your presentation, then ask yourself why would your audience think that about your presentation? And if they don't think its important, then you can be sure that they won't be listening.

Have you ever been in an audience where the speaker was talking about something that you did not think was important? Did you ever ask yourself, "So what?" Try asking yourself this very important, simple question about your presentation, and about every point that you are planning to make – "So what?" If you can't really answer that question, then think again about what you are doing.

Tip 14: Have something interesting to say	Essential

I'm sure that like me, you have sat through talks or presentations where you were simply not interested in what the speaker was trying to tell you. I have literally fallen asleep in so presentations, tutorials and seminars like that.

Having something interesting to say makes it much easier to give a great presentation. Making your audience pay attention to you and engage in your presentation will be so much easier if you have identified what interests the members of your audience and what makes them "tick". If you are talking about something that each and every member of your audience is interested in, you really cannot go too far wrong.

It really does not matter what *you* think is interesting – your presentation must address the things that *your audience* finds interesting.

Tip 15: Have something relevant to say	Essential

One incredibly effective way of making your audience engage with your presentation is to make it relevant to everyday issues that each member of your audience faces. This is where it is vital to know your audience.

Give your audience very specific, relevant examples or stories from your own life or experience with which they can identify, and show how that relates to a more general concept that can be applied in other situations that your audience faces.

It is particularly effective to talk about how your idea or concept has changed your life or your working practices. You must be a shining advocate of your own message by graphically and explicitly showing your audience how you have put your ideas into your everyday practice.

Alternatively why not frame your idea in the context of a solution – no, *the* solution – to a burning problem that your audience is experiencing. Focus your audience's attention by asking them to apply your ideas to their everyday working context, and by suggesting possible applications for what you are saying.

This really helps to drive home the practicability of your message and can set your audience's minds buzzing with imagination as they try to visualise how they can benefit or profit from your idea.

This often leads to really fruitful questions and a productive discussion after a presentation, which can benefit the speaker by giving new ideas and insights.

Tip 16: Be a leader	Intermediate

When you stand up in front of an audience and talk with them, you are in a position of leadership for the duration of your presentation. Even if your presentation is interactive and includes audience participation, fundamentally, you are still giving something of your self to your audience.

It is your role to lead your audience from an initial state of not knowing what you are going to say, to an ultimate state of having the knowledge or ideas or concepts that you have chosen to give them.

You may be apprehensive about assuming a leadership role over your audience, but to deliver an effective presentation, you will need to suppress your anxieties for the duration of the presentation and focus on the task of leadership.

You should take confidence from the fact that your audience has willingly given its authority and approval to your 30 minutes or 60 minutes of leadership. If your audience did not consent to your assuming a leadership role over them, they would not spend that time listening to you.

Tip 17: Care for your audience	Intermediate

When you plan your presentation, always be audience-centric. This means understanding your audience and making them feel understood. It means being concerned about the people in your audience, their hopes and their needs. Helping them solve their problems, achieve their goals, or fulfil their dreams through your message.

Spend less time trying to make people understand what you want. Focus on what they want. If your audience trust you and feel that you care about them, they are much more likely to cooperate with you.

Tip 18: Find common ground	Essential

Early on in your presentation you should show your audience how their needs, values, dreams and aspirations mesh with yours. This is one of the ways you can make yourself more attractive to audiences.

To do this, you need to have understood their values and concerns, and be able to see things from their point of view. If you are able to do this, you will be sympathetic with their feelings and you will be able to show them how cooperating with you can help them achieve what they want.

Tip 19: Research your topic thoroughly – be an expert	Intermediate

One of the key secrets of gaining confidence about giving your presentation is to research the topic in such a depth that you become an expert. You need to have acquired enough information about your topic that you begin to feel ownership of the topic. You must feel that you know all that there is worth knowing about the field. You need to become very familiar with the topic. You need to become very comfortable with it. It must become second nature to you, as if you have *always* known about this topic.

When you know the material and are completely comfortable with it, you will notice that your personality will be able to come out during your presentation, which is a very satisfying experience both for you as the presenter and for your audience alike. It allows you to have fun while you're talking – you will find that you are **talking about** your topic, rather than merely **presenting** it.

As part of your research, make sure that you are completely up-to-date with latest developments as well. You need to be more up-to-date in your topic than anyone else in the room.

📖 *See also:*

"Tip 26: Do not tell them everything you know", page 22
"Tip 40: Start by showing your credentials", page 30

Part C: What do you want to say?

Now is the ideal time to crystallise exactly what you want to tell your audience. Your audience's time is precious, so you owe it to them to be as focused and efficient as possible. Your message has a better chance of being accepted if it comes across clearly and cleanly.

Tip 20: Start with the end in mind	Essential

Before you even think about creating the slides or OHP transparencies, sit down and really think about the day of your presentation. What is the real purpose of your talk? Why is it that you were asked to speak? What does your audience expect? In your opinion, what are the most important parts of your topic for your audience to take away from presentation?

You should be able to write down a set of objectives for your audience. A summary of what you, as the presenter, want your audience to go home with, along with the reasons why you have selected these objectives.

(1) _____

(2) _____

(3) _____

While you are planning your presentation, keep this list of objectives displayed prominently to help you stay focused on your ultimate objectives.

Tip 21: What is your take-home message?	Essential

When you are planning your presentation, write down on a piece of paper as specifically as possible what you believe are your "take-home messages". These are the crux of your argument. These are the essence of your message. These are your thesis statements. These are your claims, your unique selling propositions.

Even if your audience forgets everything else about your presentation, you want them to remember your take-home messages. If you could tell them only a few things, what would they be?

(1) _____

(2) _____

(3) _____

Once you have written them down, keep your take-home messages handy so you can always refer to them.

Everything else about your presentation is there merely a vehicle that will allow you to deliver your take-home messages to your audience. Everything else must be built around your take-home messages.

Tip 22: Take the 60-second test	Essential

Check the clarity of your message by trying to summarise your presentation into a 60-second sound bite. Imagine that your boss has asked you to tell him the crux of your presentation in 60 seconds. Would you be able to do it?

Alternatively, try to write down the core idea for your talk as a simple sentence on the back of a business card. Try it – can you crystallize the essence of your presentation's content and write it on the back of a business card?

If you struggle with this, then you may want to get your message crystallised further in your own mind before you attempt to tell it to your audience. You should force yourself to have the discipline to get your overall message tighter and clearer.

Tip 23: What do you want your audience to do?	Essential

By now you will have an idea of what exactly you want your audience to do as a result of your presentation. Take a moment now to write this down so that you can keep this goal in the forefront of your thoughts as you plan your presentation.

> "I want my audience to approve my proposal for a new tendering process"
> "I want my audience to change the way they process application forms from new customers"
> "I want my audience to adopt my budget for the coming financial year"
> "I want my audience to approve my £100,000 grant application"
> "I want my audience to diversify their investment portfolio by buying gold bullion"
> "I want my audience to vote for my candidate"
> "I want my audience to feel angry about child poverty in Brazil"
> "I want my audience to give me a job"
> "I want my audience to give me a promotion"

As you progress through creating your presentation, keep asking yourself whether what you are including in your presentation will really bring your objectives one step closer. Can you literally visualise each slide bringing your objective closer and closer? If not, then maybe sure you are allowing your presentation to go off on a tangent, in a direction you did not originally intend.

Tip 24: What do YOU add to your presentation?	Intermediate

Once you have crystallised your objectives, identified your take-home messages and summarised your presentation into a 60-second sound bite, ask yourself whether it would be possible to write all this down in the form of a written report which you can email to your audience. Then ask yourself this question – if your audience can read all that information from a written report, what is the value of your being there in person to give this presentation?

From the point of view of your audience, the mere transfer of information from a speaker to your audience is rarely a good enough reason to have a presentation. Your audience could read the information from your report. This would be a more accurate, more reliable, faster and cheaper way of transferring the information.

So ask yourself what does YOUR being there in person add to the information transfer, which cannot be achieved as effectively by other forms of communication.

Are you hoping to inspire your audience? Are you planning to help them reach a conclusion in an interactive way? Will they have real-life questions which you can address immediately? Will you be demonstrating a skill or procedure? Are you going to entertain your audience with anecdotes or story-telling?

Think carefully about what YOU add by being there. If you cannot think of anything, then consider sending a written report instead.

Part D: How are you going to say it?

In this section we will consider some key aspects of how you will construct your presentation.

Tip 25: Keep your presentation simple	Essential

Making your presentation over-complicated is a very easy trap to fall into. Many speakers make this mistake, in an attempt to appear intelligent and knowledgeable.

In reality, giving a presentation is an entirely different genre from writing a technical report. If you are writing a report or article, you have the freedom to go into details, and the reader is at liberty to skim over sections which are not relevant, and to read the article in stages over several sittings, going over difficult areas again and again and again until they gain a satisfactory understanding.

This is not possible with a live oral presentation – your audience is not at liberty to control the flow of the interaction and so this form of communication is not suited to conveying a mass of complicated information.

➢ You do yourself and your audience a disservice by using the wrong tool for the job.

You should keep your presentation simple: have simple goals, clear messages, and moderation in length, while avoiding simplification and dumbing-down. Achieving this balance can be difficult, but it will be appreciated by your audience. It does take more forethought and planning on your part because you have to think very hard about what to include and what can be left out or conveyed better through other means.

Tip 26: Do not tell them everything you know	Essential

Do not fall into the trap of thinking that in order for your audience to understand anything, you must tell them everything.

➢ You should aim to present only 1-2% of what you know about the topic.

The remaining 98-99% should be kept in reserve. (In the real world however, it is seldom possible to have this much information held in reserve unless you are already an expert in that topic.)

Do not make your audience endure a "data dump" – this is when the presenter subjects the audience to a barrage of meaningless data in the hope that they will find something of interest somewhere in all that information. This is a sign of poor preparation as it shows that the presenter has not tailored the presentation to the interests and needs of that particular audience.

The benefit of having a large reserve of knowledge on tap is that if your audience were to ask for more information, you would be in a very strong position to deliver it. Even if your audience wanted a completely different angle from the one you had presented, you would not struggle to give your audience what they wanted.

If you're just starting out as a presenter or you're feeling insecure or you're speaking in an academic setting, your biggest temptation will be to say everything you know about your subject. Resist that temptation.

📖 *See also:*

"Tip 19: Research your topic thoroughly – be an expert", page 18

Tip 27: Organise your content

After you have decided what you want to tell your audience ar
amount of focused and relevant research, now is the time to think
data into some sort of structure. You will need to decide what yo
presentation, and what you want to leave out.

Identify what information, data and evidence is **central** to the point you want to make, and put it in one group. This is the material that will be at the core of your presentation.

Identify material that is of a **supporting** nature, and put in into a second group. You may need to call on this material later on, and it may be useful when you make a handout.

Identify material that is **peripheral** to your case. This material may be interesting to have up your sleeve but you can put this material to one side for the time being.

Tip 28: Assemble your evidence	Essential

By now you will have identified the claims or conclusions that you wish to convey to your audience. You now need to identify evidence that explains or establishes the validity of your claims.

The most commonly used forms of evidence are:

- Facts, figures, statistical evidence, graphs, charts, tables
- Stories, descriptions
- Definitions
- Historical accounts
- Case examples
- References to authority – quotations or informed opinions
- Demonstrations

Your knowledge of the audience will be crucial in deciding which form of evidence will be most credible in the eyes of your audience.

Tip 29: Have a logical, clear structure	Essential

The structure of your presentation is paramount to its success. The structure is the skeleton of your argument, and you will use it as a scaffolding to build the details of your presentation with. Without a strong structure, your content, style, delivery and great supporting visuals will fall flat.

If you took the time earlier on to outline your ideas and message and set them up in a logical fashion, then your thinking should be very clear by now. You can visualize the logic of your content and the flow of the presentation. If your ideas are not clear first, it will

possible to design the proper structure later when you create visuals and supporting
uments.

When you start to analyse great presentations by other people, you will notice that usually
the entire presentation is one big story. There is a definable **beginning**, **middle** and
ending. You should aim to emulate this highly successful and natural format of giving a
presentation.

Tip 30: Decide on the most appropriate format	Advanced

If you have a choice over the format of your presentation, think about which format will
help you to achieve your objectives for that event. It may be that you are not given the
freedom to decide on the format, and must prepare as best as you can.

➤ *Lecture*

Lecturer stands in front of an audience and talks about the subject
matter while the audience passively listens.

Advantages: A quick, cheap and traditional way of conveying a large
volume of information to a large number of people.

Disadvantages: Tedious for the audience. Difficult for participants to
ask questions or check understanding. Largely superseded by more
efficient methods of information transfer such as textbooks, the internet
and handouts. Not an effective method for promoting thought, changing
attitudes, or teaching behavioural skills.

➤ *Seminar*

Instructor leads a group of people through a discussion on a particular
subject and everyone present is requested to actively participate.

Advantages: Allows for an exchange of ideas between members of the
group. The instructor is a facilitator. Encourages critical thinking and
dialogue.

Disadvantages: The members of the group must all start with a similar
level of background knowledge. Labour-intensive and expensive.

➤ *Tutorial*

Tutor discusses a pre-defined topic with the tutorial group which is
expected to have previously researched the topic and prepared
questions and insights for discussion.

Advantages: Allows tuition to be highly customised to the learning needs of the tutorial group. The tutor can give individual attention to each student.

Disadvantages: Labour-intensive, time-consuming and expensive.

➤ *Workshop*

Expert tutors impart problem-solving skills and convey attitudes and behaviours through practical examples and exercises. Participant involvement is expected.

Advantages: Real-life situations can be explored in a controlled environment. Participants can seek solutions to their own problems from experts.

Disadvantages: Labour-intensive and expensive. Tutors possessing extensive experience and knowledge are required.

➤ *Skills teaching*

Tutors teach practical procedures through a combination of lectures, demonstrations, supervised practice, observation and examination. Hand-on audience participation.

Advantages: Allows rapid, efficient and standardised teaching of practical skills in a safe environment.

Disadvantages: Labour-intensive. Suitable training materials may be expensive. Tutors must first undergo training and assessment in the skills which are to be taught.

➤ *Role-play*

Members of the audience take turns to play different roles in pre-planned scenarios which are designed to highlight and illustrate relevant vocational learning objectives.

Advantages: Participants are able to examine and learn from their own and each other's experiences and responses to given situations.

Disadvantages: Instructors may find it a challenge to devise realistic yet controllable scenarios. Participants' behaviour in role may not reflect their real-world behaviour.

	Number in audience	Number of speakers	Audience: speaker ratio	Audience participation	Use of props	Seating arrangement
Lecture	Large	Few	High	Low	Rarely	Rows
Seminar	Medium	Few	Medium	Medium	Rarely	Semi-circular
Tutorial	Very low	Few	Low	High	Sometimes	Circular
Workshop	Medium	Several	Low	Medium	Sometimes	Groups
Skills teaching	Low	Many	Low	High	Essential	Stations
Role-play	Low	Several	Low	High	Sometimes	Variable

Tip 31: Decide the best level of audience participation	Advanced

In many circumstances, you will simply not have the freedom to decide on the level of audience participation in your presentation. However, if you are given any freedom in this matter, make sure you take full advantage of it. You are the one who will be in charge of your presentation, so you should be the one who decides on the most appropriate level of audience participation in the light of your aims & objectives and your knowledge of your audience and their learning needs.

Are you going to lecture or discuss? Will it be interactive or didactic? What aids will you use? Will members of your audience be silent recipients or will they contribute when asked or are they the main participants in your presentation?

Even if you are giving a didactic talk, this does not mean that you do not connect with your audience. If you follow the tips in this book you can still make it the most engaging presentation. Lack of participation does not necessarily mean no interaction at all.

Tip 32: Plan your presentation on paper first	Essential

Before you start making your slides, you must first plan your presentation on paper. You may use a notebook or a large sheet of blank paper. Alternatively, you may want to use a large whiteboard to sketch out your ideas. In any case, use a large enough canvas so that you feel uninhibited and free to be creative. Though you may be using digital technology when you deliver your presentation, the act of speaking and connecting to an audience – to persuade, sell, or inform – is still very much non-digital.

Planning on paper or whiteboard gives you a clear visual representation of how your content flows and inter-connects. It is much easier to stand back and get a "whole picture" view of your story when you are writing it by hand than when you are trying to write a slide.

Also, by outlining the structure of your presentation on paper or whiteboard, you will very easily be able to identify key themes and points which lend themselves to being converted into logical slides. As you write down key points and assemble an outline and structure, you can draw quick ideas for visual elements such as charts or photos that will later appear in your slides.

Planning your presentation on paper or whiteboard stimulates your creativity. There is no software to get in your way and you can easily see how the presentation and your line of argument will go. At this stage you should be dedicating all your attention to the structure, flow and objectives of your presentation, rather than being distracted by how the software works.

To create your slides or OHP transparencies before you have your key points and logical flow worked out on paper or whiteboard is like a movie director hiring actors and starting to film before there is even a script in hand!

Tip 33: Don't make your presentation too long	Essential

Most people's maximum attention span is approximately 30-45 minutes. If you exceed this limit, you'll lose your audience at the crucial point, namely your conclusion!

Audience attention is greatest at the opening and then again when you say something like "In conclusion...." So, if you have 30 minutes for your talk, finish in 25 minutes. It is better to have your audience wanting more of you than to feel that they have had more than enough.

Part E: The Beginning

First impressions are powerful. The beginning of your presentation is the first part of the presenter / audience contact. This will be the first contact you have with your audience in your role as presenter and in their role as your audience.

The first few minutes of your presentation is where your audience form perceptions of your skills, knowledge, and experience. They will make an impression of you, and that impression will profoundly affect how they see you for the rest of the session, and later on as well in any further dealings you may have. This is known as the "halo effect" or the "devil effect", depending on whether your audience sees you in a favourable light or in a negative light. Deliver a solid performance here and you will set the stage for the remainder of the session.

LENGTH OF PRESENTATION	HOW LONG IT TAKES FOR YOUR AUDIENCE TO FORM A FIRST IMPRESSION
8 minutes	1 minute
15 minute	2-3 minutes
30 minutes	4-5 minutes
60 minutes	10 minutes

➢ As a default, most audiences generally want to like the speaker, and will allow the speaker a few minutes at the beginning to engage them.

Tip 34: Establish the mood	Essential

As the beginning is the initial contact between you and your audience, it is vitally important for you to set the "mood" of your presentation. You audience will very quickly pick up on your cues, so this is the ideal time to convey to your audience whether you want the mood to be serious, happy, sombre, jovial or entertaining, for example.

Your audience will generally reflect the mood that you project onto them. If they feel you are happy, they will be happy. If they feel you are serious, they will be serious. By controlling the tone and pace of your voice, your actions, your body language and the pace of your presentation you can project onto your audience the mood that you want to create.

Tip 35: Start decisively	Essential

You should start your presentation boldly and confidently. Never start weakly. Don't apologise for being there. Don't dither. Don't be indecisive. This is not the time for your insecurities to come out!

A bad start "Errr, well, I think we should probably get started, if you want"

A better start "Hi, my name's Sandy Kennedy. It's really great to be here, and thank you so much for coming to my session. Today, we're going to talk about…"

➢ Start strong and confident, as you mean to go on.

Tip 36: Open big	Intermediate

At the time when you begin your presentation, your audience will be thinking about a whole range of different things. In the first few moments you must grab their attention and focus it on you and your presentation to the exclusion of everything else.

There are several ways to do this:

- Make some dramatic or controversial assertions
- Present a startling statistic
- Give an interesting quote

- Show an interesting slide
- Ask a question
- Quote a news headline
- Relate a pertinent anecdote

➢ Your objective is to make your audience sit up, take notice and say "Wow!"

You need to do whatever it takes to make a powerful opening with your first couple of minutes so that your audience is waiting on the edge of their seats to see what you have to say next. A strong opening assets your credibility, demonstrates your passion about the topic, and gives the impression that what you are about to say is worth listening to.

Tip 37: Start with a question	Intermediate

It is sometimes useful to start with a question that your audience would not be able to answer. You can then tell them that in the next 30 minutes time you will reveal the answer to the question. This is a powerful way of grabbing your audience's attention and motivating them to engage with you and your presentation.

Clearly, this is a more powerful technique if you link the question with the objectives of the session.

At the end of the session, ask the same question again and see if they can answer it. If you have done a good presentation, it is immensely rewarding both for you and your audience to be able to answer the question this time round. It is a practical illustration that the objectives for the session have been met.

Tip 38: Open with a personal story or anecdote	Intermediate

Another way to grab your audience's attention in the crucial few minutes at the start of your presentation is to tell them a story. People like listening to stories and it helps them to relate to you and your background. You and your audience may start out as strangers, but a personal story at the beginning of your presentation can very quickly make you seem like a trusted old friend.

You have considerable flexibility in deciding what sort of story to tell – it may be relevant to the content of your presentation, such as how this subject changed your life. Alternatively your story may be something otherwise mundane such as your journey to the event venue or something from the news. Maybe there have been problems with the transportation system in the city or particularly severe weather – this is a particularly powerful way to connect with your audience as there could be aspects to your story that they may be able to relate with.

Tip 39: Memorise your opening gambit	Essential

One technique that can really help to calm your nerves before a presentation is to memorise the first 3-5 sentences of your presentation. Practicing the opening of your presentation over and over again is really effective in helping to avoid the "opening jitters".

When you are travelling to the event venue, keep saying the first few minutes of your presentation over and over again. It doesn't always have to be 100% perfect, but when you say it for real at the start of your presentation, you will know that you have spoken those opening sentences a hundred times in the past. This can be a tremendous confidence boost.

The opening is the only part of the presentation that you should memorise or write a script for.

Tip 40: Start by showing your credentials	Essential

When you introduce yourself to your audience, you should build your credibility very early on. You must prove to them that you understand who they are, the key issues that they face, that you have done a staggering amount of homework, and that what you are about to tell them will be of interest, importance and relevance to them.

➤ You must prove to your audience that you are qualified to speak about this topic.

If you can do this, you will have secured their attention for the rest of the presentation.

Tip 41: Explain why you are worth listening to	Intermediate

As we discussed previously, the topic of your presentation should be:

- **Something that they want**
  (See: "Tip 12: Give your audience what they want", page 15)

- **Something that is important for them**
  (See: "Tip 13: Have something important to say", page 16)

- **Something that is interesting to them**
  (See: "Tip 14: Have something interesting to say", page 16)

- **Something that is relevant to them**
  (See: "Tip 15: Have something relevant to say", page 16)

A powerful way to increase your audience's attention and motivation to listen to your presentation is to explicitly spell out exactly how the thing that you are about to tell them is useful, important, interesting and relevant for them.

Tip 42: Outline your agenda at the beginning | Essential

The ancient communication principle still holds – "Tell them what you're going to say, say it, then remind them what you said."

Use the beginning of your presentation to mentally prepare your audience for learning about your topic. Give them a clear statement of the learning objectives. It sometimes helps to show a slide with an explicit list of objectives for that session.

The effect of a good talk outline is to make your audience want to hear the details and psychologically it puts them in the right mindset. At the same time, it helps them understand the structure of your thinking.

A word of warning – make sure that they outline or agenda or learning objectives that you present does actually agree with the planned structure of your talk. It is no good telling your audience that you will proceed in a particular direction, but then divert along the way and end up in a completely different destination!

Tip 43: Use the beginning to bring everyone up to speed | Essential

Members of your audience will typically come from different backgrounds and all may not come with the same level of baseline knowledge. It is vitally important to make sure they are all at the same level before you try to deliver your message. So use the beginning of your presentation to give background information and bring everyone in your audience to the same level.

Your understanding of your audience's background will be crucial for you to work out where to start from – you need to know what knowledge is a common denominator and can therefore be assumed, and what knowledge may not be universal.

Don't worry about boring those who already have the basic knowledge – your introduction can provide a useful revision for those who already know, and most importantly, it provides them with confirmation that *you* have the basic understanding that is required for them to take *you* seriously.

You should also use the beginning to set the context of your presentation, to lay the foundation of what you will build in the middle part of the presentation.

Tip 44: Define roles	Advanced

You will have decided a long time ago what roles you and the members of your audience will play in your presentation (*see "Tip 31: Decide the best level of audience participation", page 26*). For example, you would have decided whether your audience would be active or passive, or whether you are expecting to ask them questions or give them tasks to perform.

You should use the beginning to openly define the roles of presenter and audience, so that your audience knows from the outset what is expected of them. You can do this with simple statement and body language. Also, the layout of the room and seating pattern would have already told them about the expected participation levels.

Part F: The Middle

The middle is the main crux of your presentation. This is where you tell your audience what you want to tell them. This is where you develop your argument. This is where you show your facts. Naturally, it is the largest and most significant part of the session.

This is the part of the presentation where you must make sure your content is conveyed to your audience in a clear and logical form, at a level which can be understood.

Tip 45: Give your audience a way of tracking progress	Intermediate

Have you ever had to endure a presentation where the speaker just went on and on and on, and you were getting frustrated because you didn't know when he or she was going to end? I certainly have, on many occasions. And it's not necessarily because the speaker was bad or the topic was boring – this can happen even if the presentation is otherwise good.

Your audience naturally wants to know how much longer the presentation will last for. If the speaking slot is a fixed time such as 15 minutes at a conference, then they can keep track with the watch. Otherwise it can be very frustrating to not know whereabouts in the presentation you are.

One simple way to avoid this problem is to give your audience an easy way to know where you are in your presentation. Title your talk in such a way that your audience knows how long you will be speaking for. For example – if the title of you presentation is "7 strategies for market capitalisation in a globalised economy", and you are talking about strategy number 4, then your audience will know that you are roughly half-way through.

📖 *See also:*

"*Tip 141: Include a presentation progress tracker*", page 84

Tip 46: Focus on main arguments rather than details	Intermediate

Especially in a conference situation where each speaker is given a short, fixed allocation of minutes and there are many presentations taking place in the space of a few hours, you cannot expect to convey all the relevant information about your subject in that time, and you cannot expect your audience to absorb every minutiae of data that you present to them. In such a situation, less is more.

Give your audience short, striking punch lines that they'll remember. Your presentation should be like a TV advert, advertising your written article or research, or to generate contacts for future collaboration. It should stimulate your audience's curiosity so that they will read your article or get in touch with you personally.

Tip 47: Give them the facts	Essential

If you want to convince your audience of your message, make sure you back up your argument with facts, evidence and proof. Take care to select the data and visual tools that will support the point you are making, whether it is with statistics, graphs or charts.

Be careful however that you do not overwhelm your audience with too much information – there is a subtle line between too much and too little information. There is a skill in being able to select the appropriate information that will support your case, without giving so much information that your audience cannot digest it or make sense of it.

Tip 48: Use concrete examples	Essential

A powerful way to convince your audience of your argument is to give them concrete examples that they can understand, relate to, believe in and latch on to. Talk about individual projects or cases where your point has been demonstrated. Show how your idea solved particular problems. Your conclusions are much more credible when backed up with great success stories.

You may want to bring along a satisfied customer who can stand up for 2-3 minutes and testify to the success your ideas have created. Alternatively, bring along a working demonstration of the product you are talking about.

Tip 49: Use quotations	Advanced

Have you ever found yourself making a bold statement in your presentation, and then looking around your audience and getting the sinking feeling when you realise that they don't really believe what you are trying to say...? I've been there.

If what you are saying goes contrary to your audience's experience, beliefs or expectations, they have a simple choice – either they can take your statement at face value or they can simply refuse to believe you.

One useful technique for such situations is to use a quotation that backs up your statement, made by someone who your audience knows and can relate to and believe in.

When you use a quotation, you suddenly and unexpectedly give your audience a third and viable option – to believe someone who they trust (other than you!). Using a quotation can make your point more credible in an instant.

Apart from industry-specific quotations, you should aim to build a collection of generic quotations that you can use in a variety of situations. The following websites are a useful starting point for your collection:

http://www.wikiquote.org
http://www.brainyquote.com
http://www.thinkexist.com

Alternatively, simply use your favourite internet search engine with a search query such as "quotes about economics"

Tip 50: Obey the NATYAUTSATYD rule	Essential

Always obey the NATYAUTSATYD rule –

> "**N**ever **A**ssume **T**hat **Y**our **A**udience **U**ses **T**he **S**ame **A**cronyms **T**hat **Y**ou **D**o"

➢ Make sure you define each acronym the first time you use it.

Tip 51: Let your audience arrive at your conclusion	Advanced

When you are trying to convince your audience, build up your argument sequentially until the conclusion you are trying to convey is obvious for your audience. You should allow them to arrive at your conclusion. Let them work it out. You may want to suggest the answer indirectly, but do let them believe that they are always one step ahead of you.

Your audience must reach your conclusion before you spell it out, so they will say "I knew that."

➢ Making your audience "own" your conclusion is a subtle but potent and ever-so-slightly devious way of getting your audience to accept your point.

Tip 52: Summarize the story periodically	Intermediate

When you write a report or article, you can expect the reader to follow one line of thought for approximately 20-30 minutes before his or her mind starts to lose track of the plot.

This is because the reader has the option to re-read certain sections, or to jump around in a block of text. The reader is in control of the flow of information and can direct the flow in accordance with his or her needs and understanding.

However, when you are giving an oral presentation, you are in control of the flow of information, not your audience. So you cannot expect them to keep track of one train of thought for more than 10-15 minutes.

You can get around this by letting your audience know the outline of your presentation at the outset, and by periodically cycling back to the outline, stepping back to get a global view of the progress of your presentation, and reminding them of where the presentation is going.

Tip 53: Break up long presentations	Advanced

Your audience can concentrate for only small periods of time – far smaller than the length of most talks. Therefore you must incorporate natural landmarks in your presentation where your audience can either take a pause completely or switch focus to another subject.

There are several ways of doing this, depending on whether you want a subtle change in focus to liven up audience interest, or whether you want a complete pause.

BREAK REQUIRED	TECHNIQUE
Small	Signpost your important messages so that the audience notices a change in topic. Change the style and pace (use crescendos and decrescendos, fortissimos pianissimos, staircases and landings) of your delivery. Tell a story, a light-hearted illustration or anecdote, use examples, make comparisons. Surprise your audience.
Medium	Step back to the objectives, to get a global picture or bird's eye view of where you are going. Take some questions from the audience. Take a couple of minutes to load a new set of slides.
Large	Take a 5-10 minute break to allow the audience to walk about / stretch / go to toilet / get a drink.
Major	Have an audience participation session.

Part G: The Ending

The end is the conclusion of your presentation. It is the grand finale. It is the happy ending. It is the call to action. It is the take-home message delivered on a plate. You need to think carefully about how you will end your presentation and how your audience will remember you after you have gone. If you don't end clearly, but just peter out, this has an unsatisfactory and unprofessional feel about it and may leave unanswered questions in your audience's mind.

You want to close strong as people are more likely to remember the last thing you said rather than the detail in the middle of your presentation.

Tip 54: Summarise your presentation at the end	Essential

"Tell them what you're going to say, say it, then remind them what you said" – now that you have said what you wanted to say, it is worthwhile telling your audience what you think you have said and how your initial objectives have been met.

A concise summary helps your audience comprehend your main points and relate different areas together. It helps you to tie-up any loose ends. Some members of your audience may not have been paying attention during your presentation, or have failed to keep up with the flow of your presentation. It is therefore worthwhile using the summary as a reinforcement of what you wanted them to take from your presentation.

Tip 55: End on a high	Intermediate

Always plan to end your presentation on a positive note. Your audience will remember your entire audience as being positive, if you are able to end with positive words and thoughts. Maybe tell a light-hearted anecdote, or a joke. Possibly show a humorous slide or a slide with a cartoon. Be imaginative, but also make sure you are faithful and congruent with the overall style of your presentation.

Tip 56: Have a call to action	Advanced

Your presentation is an advertisement – whether you are advertising your ideas for others to buy, or whether you are advertising your product or your research. No advertisement is worth anything if there is no call to action. If you don't inspire or challenge your audience to do something, then why speak to them?

When you have finished your presentation, your audience must be inspired, challenged and motivated to do something amazing with the new information they have learned from you.

It helps to offer your audience a practical action plan – something that they can start or accomplish in the next 72 hours. This cements their commitment to your message, and illustrates its practicality.

Tip 57: Have a definite termination	Intermediate

The termination is literally the final contact you have with your audience. There are several ways to achieve a satisfactory and decisive termination.

- Thank your audience, break eye contact and physically move away from the public arena.

- Ask your audience to get up and go somewhere or do something.

- Hand over to next speaker.

You should try to plan your termination in advance, bearing in mind the circumstances of the event and programme.

Tip 58: Thank your audience	Essential

It is a courtesy to thank the event organisers who asked you to come, and to thank your audience for listening.

Tip 59: Take questions from your audience	Intermediate

If your presentation was stimulating and interesting for your audience, they will probably have thought of some questions. Now is a great time for you to take those questions and answer them.

> 📖 *See also:*
>
> *"Chapter 9: 'Any questions?", page 137*

Part H: Connect with your audience

As the speaker, you must "connect" with your audience as soon as possible, preferably in the first 60 seconds of your presentation. After you have connected, you must work to maintain that connection throughout the presentation.

But what does it mean to "connect"? It means you must be on the same wavelength. It means you must have a rapport. It means you must win their trust. It means that you understand everything about them, and they understand everything about you. It means that there are no barriers between you and them.

➢ To connect is to have an almost spiritual relationship between the presenter and the audience.

If you want your audience to hear what you say, take it in and respond in the way you want them to, they need to feel that you care about them and their needs. When you care about people, they respond.

Tip 60: Tell some stories	Advanced

Using stories, illustrations, vignettes and anecdotes is a fantastic way of establishing a relationship with your audience. Good speakers are good storytellers and audiences can relate to them in a way they won't relate to anything else.

These are some of the benefits of using stories in your presentations:

- Telling a story about something that affects you is a good way for you to relax at the start of a presentation

- People are naturally drawn in by real stories. Whenever a speaker starts to tell a story, everyone in the audience immediately wakes up to hear it.

- It makes your talk natural. When you tell a story, you're not "making a speech" anymore. You're simply having a conversation.

- Stories are real-life examples which illustrate your point. The easiest way to explain complicated ideas is through examples or by sharing a story that underscores the point. Great speakers tell stories that support their message.

- People remember stories. If you want your audience to remember your message, then find short, interesting stories or examples to support your major points.

You must be imaginative and unique when you tell your stories. Talk about your youth. Tell a story about your kids. Stories about your customers. Stories about things in the news. Even if it's made up, it'll keep your audience interested and keep the presentation topic grounded in something practical and realistic.

Good stories have interesting, clear beginnings, provocative, engaging content in the middle, and a clear, logical conclusion. Tell relevant stories in a clear, concise manner.

Tip 61: Respect your audience	Essential

Being at the front of an audience of people can give some speakers such a sense of power and authority that they come across as arrogant, condescending, disdainful or cocky.

➢ This is not appropriate.

When you are speaking, you must be dignified and humble. Never allow yourself to feel superior to anyone else in the audience. They will not appreciate you for it and you will almost certainly be embarrassed about it afterwards.

The group of people in front of you has been winnowed down from all the people in the world by a complicated and elaborate process. Even if they are junior to you, you should treat them as at least your equals and peers, if not higher than that. They deserve your utmost respect and should be treated as favoured guests.

Tip 62: Entertain your audience	Advanced

Sometimes we make a presentation that communicates the arguments and evidence, and then persuades your audience that they are true, and we naturally assume that because of this, it will be interesting and entertaining and will therefore hold the audience's attention. Sometimes we even scoff at the idea of giving an interesting and entertaining presentation – we seem to think that if a talk is entertaining, it's probably not very "deep".

This is not necessarily the case. In fact, it is impossible to communicate and persuade effectively without entertaining at the same time. If people are entertained, you can slip in a few nuggets of information. But if your speech is dull and boring, no amount of information will make it a great speech.

Keeping your audience interested and involved is essential because in order to communicate your work and its value, you need their full attention.

Listening is hard work. Especially at conferences, where audiences listen to many talks over many hours, people need the speaker's help to maintain their focus.

Entertainment isn't about making your audience laugh or distracting them from their troubles, but simply about keeping them focused on and interested in what you have to say.

Surprise, delight, challenge, and engage your audience. People are busy – if they can get the same info from a book or an email, why bring them in to listen to a presentation?

Tip 63: Be different	Advanced

Successful speakers are memorable because they are different from the rest. They aren't like everybody else. There's something that sets them apart, makes them stand out. They are the speakers who do more than just stand in the front of the room and talk at you.

Don't be different just for the sake of it or to be remembered as the joker in the pack. But for example, in the endless row of presentations at a conference, try to do something completely unique. This could be in the context of the design of your slides, your examples or your stories for example.

Tip 64: Tell a secret about yourself	Advanced

Telling a secret about yourself in public involves risk and vulnerability. But this is a nice way of opening up to an audience of strangers, as it makes them feel you are so confident about yourself and your role as a presenter and leader, that you are able to tell a personal secret to the group. In response to this, your audience will naturally reciprocate by feeling more relaxed about opening up to you.

Mildly embarrassing self-deprecation is especially appreciated – people can relate to it, and it makes your talk relevant to them.

Tip 65: Get personal with your audience	Advanced

This is a very strong tactic when giving speeches. Tie your speech into one of your real life experiences. Make your audience feel the warmth or feel as if they are your best friend.

Sharing information about yourself is a quick way to win over your audience. You may get different feedback about this point, but try and make eye contact with your audience. It helps your audience better associate themselves with you. It makes your speech more personal.

Tip 66: Let your personality shine through	Intermediate

You should allow your personality to come across in your presentations. Let it shine through. It is one of the things that will most differentiate you from other speakers – no one wants you to be a clone.

Tip 67: Challenge your audience	Advanced

A powerful way of engaging with your audience is to challenge them to take what you give them in the presentation and go and do great things with it.

Tip 68: Use a conversational style of talking	Intermediate

If you want to connect and develop a strong rapport with your audience, you need to talk like a human being. Speak in a language and style of conversation that will make it easier for your audience to understand you. Don't hide behind complicated words or vaguely defined phrases, except in the context of a technical presentation. Try to use simple, human, everyday words whenever possible. Don't try to show off by using corporate-speak. It may impress some, but you won't win over your audience with it.

You are not a robot or a computer or a machine! Talk like an ordinary human being. It is easier to understand, and it allows you to make genuine contact with your audience. Talk as if you are talking with your best friend or spouse. Have a real, frank, informal chat among friends, rather than putting on a fake corporate veneer. Successful speakers involve their audiences and converse with them so that it's a conversation, not a talking-to. Talk what matters to you in your own words with your own passion and you will gain your audience's attention.

Tip 69: Be positive	Essential

No matter what the subject or the circumstances of your presentation, you should always meet your audience with a positive frame of mind, and come across as being positive.

Even if you have had a bad day, don't take it out on your audience. They aren't to blame for your car breaking down or the problems you're having with your teenage kids!

Even if you are presenting bad news, try to focus on the silver lining. It will make your presentation more palatable and constructive.

Part I: Make your presentation interactive

Adults can learn better and retain knowledge longer when they have an active part in the learning process. Research has shown that interactivity and audience participation are essential for effective adult learning.

Interactivity breaks down the barrier between speaker and audience. You should always aim to conduct interactive lectures, and think of your audience as being active participants rather than passive listeners.

Even if you are giving a didactic lecture, there are ways of introducing a level of interactivity with your audience which your audience will appreciate.

Tip 70: Tools for interactivity	Intermediate

These are some of the commonly used ways of encourage active audience participation:

- Asking your audience to think about something, or imagine a scenario, or think for a moment about what they would do in a given situation.

- Asking rhetorical questions – you are not expecting them to reply to you, but they should take a moment to think about how they would respond to your question.

- Asking for a show of hands.

- Asking simple questions. Answers may be taken from individual members of your audience, or your audience may shout out the answers.

- Asking the audience to individually write down answers to a question, and then comparing with a model answer that you give. The answer can be given immediately, or at the end of the presentation.

- Ask for a volunteer to take part in a demonstration – ask members of the audience to come to the podium with you.

- Asking a "trick question" which the audience would be expected to be able to answer, but giving an answer that is different from what the audience expected.

- Group exercises.

- Role-playing exercises.

- Spending 5 minutes taking questions from the audience after every 20-30 minutes of presentation.

- Ask the audience to think practical applications for the information they are being presented with.

- Asking the audience to reflect on their own practice and share best practice with the group.

- Involving the audience in identifying learning needs for that session and setting goals by negotiation – the speaker's experience can be invaluable to help the audience set realistic goals.

Tip 71: Use a whiteboard, blackboard or flip chart	Advanced

If you have access to a whiteboard & dry marker or blackboard & chalk or flip chart & marker pen, you can use these to engage your audience in your presentation. These are useful tools to openly note down and interact with contributions from the audience.

A word of caution though – it does require some practice to be able to write legibly on a vertical surface, and you must master the skill beforehand!

Also, you should make sure your writing is neat and legible. It needs to be large enough to be read from the back of the room otherwise you will be excluding a number of people who simply cannot read it from the distance. Do carry a spare whiteboard pen or chalk or marker pen in case you run out.

The advantage of using a whiteboard or blackboard is that you can easily modify the text or diagrams during the course of the session. The advantage of a flip chart is that you can go back to something that was written earlier on.

Be careful not to use any of these media as your scribbling pad during the course of the discussion, or your audience may become confused!

Part J: Prepare for questions

Planning for a question & answer session is part of the preparation for your presentation.

Tip 72: Prepare for questions	Essential

If you will be asked questions at the end, try to choose a topic that you know well enough that you can answer reasonable questions while *sounding* intelligent, knowledgeable and authoritative.

As you prepare your presentation, make a list of the toughest questions that you might be asked and write down their answers. When you've prepared for the worst questions, the rest seems easy.

Tip 73: Plant a question	Advanced

Clearly, you would prefer to be asked questions that you can answer, and you do not want to be open to any questions you cannot answer. It may be possible to direct the nature of the questions that you will be asked.

Try to say something slightly foolish or outrageous or controversial during your talk – a "deliberate mistake". If your audience notices, someone will surely want to quiz you about it. Have your answer ready and your question & answer session will go a lot smoother.

If you have not planted a question like this, the chairperson would be *compelled* out of politeness, courtesy and etiquette to think hard and come up with at least *one* question. If you are unlucky, it may be a difficult question!

📖 *See also:*

"*Tip 263: Have your own questions ready*", page 139

Part K: Be a giver

"Ask not what your audience can do for you; ask what you can do for your audience"

Tip 74: Give them something	Essential

When you are preparing your presentation, you should not be thinking about what your audience or this presentation can do for you. Don't think about the fame, or the promotion, or the pay rise, or the status, or the contract that will come as a result of this presentation.

➤ Throughout the presentation and the preparation, ask yourself – "What am I *giving*? How can I give *more*?"

The simple secret is that the more you give your audience, the more you get back from your audience and the presentation.

Tip 75: Give your audience access to materials	Intermediate

You want your audience to feel that they have joined an exclusive club of people who have had the privilege & opportunity to experience your presentation. This will make them value your effort and the significance of your message even more.

A good way of doing this is to allow them access to materials such as your slides, data and supporting materials.

You can ask those who are interested in receiving these materials to write their email addresses down and then emailing it to them, as long as the file size is not too big.

Alternatively, a very effective technique for generating interest is to burn materials onto a small number of CD-ROMs and give them to any interested audience members. If you need more CD-ROMs, take a note of postal addresses and promise to send them CD-ROMs by post.

If you have a website or blog, you can also upload materials for people to access.

Part L: Plan for failure

"The day you forget your umbrella, it pours with rain"
– A variation of Murphy's law

Tip 76: Have a backup plan available	Essential

When you are using technology in your presentation, you must always have a backup plan in case the technology is not available unexpectedly. Something can, and often does, go wrong with the computer, the projector, the software, the cables, the power supply or your presentation itself.

You must do everything possible to get yourself back on your feet in the fact of technical failure:

- Save your presentation on alternative storage devices – on USB sticks and onto a writable CD-ROM, and take them with you.

- Save your presentation in different formats such as PDF or Word.

- If you have web mail account such as Hotmail.com or Yahoo! Mail or Gmail, email yourself a copy of your presentation and leave it in your inbox. If you need to access your presentation from a foreign venue it will be in your inbox.

- Take a print out of your slides or OHP transparencies – one sheet of A4 paper for each slide.

Despite all these measures, always be mentally prepared to deliver your talk without any slide, transparencies or props, just in case. Your presentation and your message are too important to be cut short due to technical failure: the show must go on!

Tip 77: Take photos of your equipment with you	Intermediate

If you are travelling to a foreign country for your presentation, you may find that you don't actually know the Romanian word for "slide projector" or the Venezuelan word for "laser pointer" or the Mongolian word for "computer". How do you say "I need a power cable for my laptop" in Xhosa?

Rather than fumbling through your phrase-book at the last minute, it is far easier and less stressful to simply pack photos of the key equipment you require for your presentation. You can either take the photos yourself, or cut them out of a trade magazine.

Then when you need to ask an Uzbek shopkeeper in Tashkent for a 240V AC power adapter, it hopefully won't turn into a Central Asian game of charades.

Chapter 2: Preparing the delivery

"Without wonder and insight, acting is just a trade.
With it, it becomes creation."
– Bette Davis (1908-1989), American actress

Although you will have researched your topic as thoroughly as possible, the way you delivery your presentation will play a key factor in whether it will ultimately be successful

Tip 78: Avoid having to dim the lights	Essential

People often say that you should dim the lights when you begin your presentation so that your audience can see your slides better. In fact, in some cultures, it is considered good manners and a sign of great respect towards the speaker for a member of the audience to dim the lights when the presentation begins.

There are several problems with this though. First and foremost, allowing the lights to be dimmed at the start of the presentation sends a strong message to your audience that the key focus of the presentation is the slides. It elevates the slides to a position higher than the person presenting them. The slides assume an importance greater than the human being who is delivering the presentation. Your audience understands that you are giving preference to your slides over yourself – you are dimming the lights so that the *slides* can be seen at the expense of being seen yourself. You are giving a non-verbal cue to your audience which states that they should be focusing on the slides rather than on you.

This should not normally be the case. Your audience came to see you, to hear you, to interact with you, to discuss with you, to benefit from your presence. The slides should be a tool for you. They should be subservient to you, your aims and your objectives. Your audience should be looking at you more than the screen.

When you dim the lights, you are hiding in the dark. Non-verbal communication is a very important part of the skill-set of the successful speaker. When you dim the lights, you make it much more difficult for you to project non-verbal cues onto your audience. In particular, your facial expressions will be very difficult to see. You put yourself at an immediate disadvantage when you dim the lights, because connecting with, engaging and persuading your audience suddenly becomes harder.

Also, when you dim the lights, you make it harder for you to read any written notes or prompts that you may have. Just as your audience cannot see you, you cannot pick up on your audience's non-verbal feedback cues. You may also help your audience fall asleep when the lights are low, especially if you are presenting straight after lunch!

The bad habit of turning lights down started in the days of 35mm slides and slide projectors which were not really bright enough to be seen with the lights on. Today's modern projectors are usually bright enough to be used comfortably without dimming the lights.

The only real reason to dim the lights is when the detail of a technical image is too important to miss. You should then dim the lights while displaying the image, and then put them on again when you move to the next slide.

Tip 79: Keep your sentences simple	Essential

You should talk in a conversational style, as if you are talking amongst old friends. Keep the style of your talking natural and relaxed. By doing so, you build a natural and human rapport with your audience.

Avoid using long, complex sentences, or sentences filled with jargon. This builds barriers between people and distances you from your audience unnecessarily.

Tip 80: Be bold	Intermediate

When you are in the public arena as a leader trying to convince an audience of your argument, you need to be bold in your style of talking, your expressions, your body language, your eye contact and your mannerisms. You bring forward the most watertight case but you cannot hope to convince your audience of anything if you come across as weak, timid or mediocre.

Take ownership of the message you are conveying, be bold, tell what you believe to be the truth, and be prepared to justify it.

Tip 81: Don't deceive your audience	Essential

Sometimes you may be tempted to fake your expert status, or to pass as truths things which you know are lies.

While you may be able to deceive individuals in private conversations, do not attempt to do this in the public arena. You *will* get exposed and the consequences could be disastrous. Audiences are far more perceptive than most people give them credit for, are quick to condemn and slow to forgive.

Tip 82: Draw a diagram	Advanced

Drawing a diagram in real-time during your presentation is a relatively underused but remarkably effective way of engaging with your audience and getting your point across. In effect, you start with a blank canvas and graphically construct your argument in front of your audience's very eyes.

You already know that "a picture is worth a thousand words"... but you can reveal an entirely new dimension of information about inter-relationships, sequences, priorities and dependencies, if you can deconstruct that thousand-word picture and show your audience how to put it back together again. It is a very powerful way to interact with your audience.

You can draw a diagram in several ways. Traditionally, you can draw your diagram on a blackboard, whiteboard or flip-chart. Alternatively you can sequentially build a slide presentation, adding elements to the diagram in successive slides.

📖 *See also:*

"Tip 142: Use object builds", page 85

Tip 83: Know what you are presenting	Essential

Sometimes you will be asked to give a presentation where the presentation slide set will be given to you by someone else. At other times, you may find yourself giving a presentation that you have already previous given to a different audience. The mistake some speakers make in this situation is to assume that all the hard work has already been done.

This is a dangerous attitude, because you do both yourself and your audience a great disservice if you stand up to give your presentation without knowing the presentation as thoroughly as if you had only recently created it specifically for that audience yourself.

Even if you are given individual slides or a slide-set to present, you still have the scope to select, prioritise or otherwise emphasise elements of the content, based on your knowledge of audience, their background, experience and needs.

You must take time to get to know the content of your presentation. Know the supporting data for any ideas you will present. Think about the questions that may arise from this audience. Find ways of personalising the presentation for this unique audience. Rehearse the presentation as many times as you can, exactly as if you were giving it for the first time.

Tip 84: Target your audience's emotions	Advanced

When you are giving your presentation, you are talking with human beings. You will be surprised how many people forget this and think they are talking to a wall! Or talking to computers or machines. Inexperienced or nervous speakers often fail to realise that they are talking to ordinary people who live with both intellect and emotion. Often, a person's emotional response can produce more striking results than an intellectual or theoretical response.

Even if you are giving a technical presentation, it should not be a pure data presentation alone. If you want your audience to "feel" something about your data you will need to address their feelings and present your pitch in a way that they feel motivated to accept it.

Tip 85: Don't use the same format as your thesis	Essential

When you are presenting your academic paper to a live audience, do not present it in the same format as you have used to write your paper. "Abstract, Introduction, Hypothesis, Aims, Methods, Results, Conclusions" may be suitable chapter headings for your thesis, but your presentation should not be merely a reading aloud of your thesis or research paper.

Presentations are not articles or theses. They are a completely different medium of communication, and they require a different set of skills. This fact is often not grasped by researchers or students. Written academic language is simply too awkward for reading aloud. If your audience wanted to read your article, you could have emailed it to them and saved everyone a lot of time, effort and expense! The aim of your presentation is not to read your paper out loud.

Have a think about exactly what you want your audience to gain from your presentation. Do you want them to go away and read your paper? Do you want them to learn about your conclusions and use them to advance their own research? Do you want them to share their thoughts on your research or give you ideas to improve it? Are you making a pitch for funding or employment? Do you want to attract new students to your department?

Use your presentation to achieve whatever objectives you want. The paper is merely an excuse for you to get out there in front of an attentive audience and talk. Use it to create a spark, a connection between you and your audience, to move them towards whatever goal you have set.

Tip 86: Add some relevant humour	Advanced

If you can carefully incorporate some humour into the flow of your presentation, this can be a very useful way to keep your audience's interest and rapport. Adults may learn better and be more receptive to your ideas when the mood is light.

Having humour does not just mean jokes. There are so many ways to introduce humour to lighten the load of an otherwise heavy presentation without restricting yourself to jokes. In any case, jokes can be dangerous as some members of your audience may not "get" the joke and you may find them alienated unnecessarily. You need to know your audience really well to know which jokes would work and which would fall flat, embarrassing both you and your audience. If you are going to use jokes, use them against yourself and never against other others – "I am the joke" is the safest approach when making a joke.

Use your imagination to think of ways of adding humour, depending on your own skills and confidence. Use the extremes of your life to build humour in your story telling. Many points which are actually profoundly deep can be illustrated by a good cartoon or photograph with or without a caption. It may be better for you to provide the caption in real time. If you are able, there may also be a place for some magic tricks, handwriting analysis, or a song in your presentation, although you do have to be totally confident in delivering these things if you want your audience to be totally at ease while receiving them.

Remember that there are tremendous cross-cultural variations in sense of humour and in norms related to gender, sexuality, politics, race and religion. Humour that is intentionally or accidentally disrespectful, confrontational or reveals your prejudices must be avoided as it can alienate your audience without good reason.

If you are going to use humour but your audience is not expecting it, it is sometimes a good idea to first give them permission to laugh! Tell them up front to enjoy themselves, or that you are about to tell a joke, and they will be more receptive to your style of presentation. If a boss is present amongst a group of peers, bear in mind that the audience may not laugh until they see the boss lighten up and give them permission to appreciate your humour.

Be careful if you are planning to open your presentation with humour: if the humour does not work, your entire presentation will have been started on the wrong foot. It is therefore best to avoid opening with a joke unless you know you're the type of person who can tell jokes in public.

Tip 87: Use props	Advanced

In public speaking the term "prop" is a shortened version of the theatrical term "property," a word used to describe any object handled or used by an actor in a performance.

Props can be an incredibly powerful way to liven up your presentation and make it more memorable. Props help focus attention on the speaking points you are trying to make along with illustrating them for you. They make better connections than your words with the visually oriented members of your audience. They create interest, add variety, and make your points more memorable. Many times a well selected prop will illustrate your point much better than you could ever do in words. Your audience can easily ignore your words, but a unique prop is hard to ignore.

People remember pictures far longer than words. That is why great public speakers use stories to create images in their audience's mind. They know that images will be remembered when the words are long forgotten. If you are not a great storyteller yet, you can use props to help create these pictures at your presentations.

Normally you should keep your props hidden until you are ready to use them: props are at their most potent when the audience does not know about their existence until the moment when they interrupt the flow of the presentation.

If you do use props, make sure they can be seen from all parts of the room and that you continue to speak to your audience and not to the prop (unless the prop is a puppet).

Tip 88: Don't use a written script	Intermediate

Many speakers, especially those who are nervous about speaking in public or are inexperienced, write a complete script of their entire presentation. I would strongly advise against such a strategy! It will be easily apparent to your audience that you are reading from a script, and this simply exposes your inconfidence or inexperience. Writing your speech really is a last resort.

In most situations, as long as you know your presentation thoroughly, you should be able to manage with writing short bullet points for each point you want to make. These will act as your aide-memoirs or road signs along the way. Make up the gaps between the bullet points as you go. This comes across as more natural and makes you seem more confident.

It is acceptable to have an outline of your presentation slides and notes on the desk in front of you, or even in your hand. But don't go as far as using a written script.

> 📖 *See also:*
>
> *"Tip 151: Make some notes for yourself", page 89*

Tip 89: Don't memorize your presentation	Intermediate

Apart from memorising the opening sentences of your presentation, you should avoid memorising the rest of the presentation like a speech.

Firstly, it is usually obvious to the audience that you are reciting a memorised speech because the natural pauses, intonations and variations of speed and tone that occur in real-life conversation are lost. You sound like a machine and that puts a barrier between you and your human audience.

Secondly, if someone interrupts you to ask a question while you are talking, you will have to answer the question and while you are answering the unplanned question you will be talking in your natural conversational mode. Your audience will immediately and very easily notice the two distinct modes of talking – one natural, and one fake. Believe me, this looks really odd and your audience will wonder why you can't just talk to them like a human being rather than subjecting them to your dry, wooden, pre-prepared speech!

Then you will have to resume your memorised speech from where you left off. This is not normally something you will have planned for, and most people who have memorised their speech do a terrible job of picking up from where they left off and finding the flow of their speech. Again, the difference in style of talking between the speech and the question & answer interaction is almost tangible. Your audience will be left wanting to know more about the real you that they glimpsed in the unplanned window in your presentation.

Don't memorize your speech word for word. Commit your message to heart and commit yourself to speaking your truth. Memorize your outline, the flow and structure of your speech. And memorize, if you can, the opening and closing words of your speech. If you need help, prepare some simple outline notes to speak from, and take them to the front of the room with you.

Tip 90: Don't read out your presentation slides	Intermediate

As you are making your slides, keep asking yourself one question. If someone who isn't at your presentation were to see your slides, could they understand your presentation? If the answer is yes, then you have got a big problem with your slides.

If a person who isn't there can understand your presentation by just reading your slides, then what you are adding by being there in person? You audience can read your slides in the printed conference book or on the CD when it arrives.

If you don't really need to be there, then why bother? Why spend your money and time travelling to the venue at all? Why should your audience spend their time listening to you?

If you are there to read some bullet points from a projector screen then don't go. Email your bullet points to your audience and let them read through them themselves. It will be more efficient because people read faster than they can speak or listen.

The fact that the presenter is there in person is the most important feature of giving a presentation rather than writing an article. I have watched too many presentations where this advantage has been wasted. Presentations where a person goes on stage, reads through a bunch of bullet points and goes off stage.

➢ Don't read your presentation from the screen. Your audience is perfectly capable of reading the presentation, they don't need it read for them.

	Article	Presentation
Interaction	Limited	Strong
Opportunity to test audience's understanding	Low	High
Emotional link	No	Yes
2-way conversation	No	Yes

Differences between an article and an oral presentation

Tip 91: Face your audience	Essential

Whenever you give a presentation, always remember that the focus of the presentation is you, and not your slide set. Always be in a position where you will be facing your audience. Talk to your audience, not to the projection screen.

Never be one of those speakers who sits at the front of the room facing the projection screen with his back towards the audience and fails to notice that the entire audience has fallen asleep behind him!

Always make sure that you are positioned such that you can achieve the following three rules simultaneously:

- Face your audience, so that you can see them and they can see you.

- See which slide your audience is seeing, so that you can check you are on the correct slide.

- See your notes, either on the desk in front of you or in your hand.

Sometimes getting this juggling act does take some advance planning and practice. You should aim to face your audience at least 80% of the time. Avoid turning your back to your audience.

Tip 92: Stand, rather than sit	Intermediate

Your audience needs to see you at all times during your presentation. So unless you are literally forced to sit down by etiquette or physical disability, you should try to stand whenever you can. Your audience will see you better, and standing puts you in a more dominant and influential position.

You are the focus of your presentation, not your slides or your handouts. Your audience needs you to be in charge of your presentation and standing up will help you achieve this naturally.

Tip 93: Move, rather than stand still	Advanced

It is easier for your audience to maintain focus on a moving target rather than trying to concentrate on a fixed spot. So, during your presentation you should move around the podium, if not around the room itself. Even if you are constrained by convention to standing in a fixed spot such as at a lectern, you can achieve a similar effect by periodically changing the direction that your body is facing.

It would be easy to overdo this movement, so be careful that your movements around the room don't distract people from the content of your presentation. Don't pace up and down the room! Make sure that you walk around naturally as it suggests you are feeling at ease with both your surroundings and the material.

Tip 94: Vary the pitch of your voice	Intermediate

The pitch of your voice increases and decreases in natural conversation. Without even thinking about it, we use this change in pitch to emphasise certain points, and to deemphasise others. This helps the person we are talking with better understand what we are saying.

However, many speakers, especially when they are nervous or are reading a pre-prepared script, speak in a monotonous drone which is very annoying for your audience to listen to. It is so unnatural to listen to that it actually makes it harder for your audience to understand what you are saying as the natural cues suggested by the pitch of your voice are completely lost.

Further, if you continue in a monotonous voice for any length of time, your audience will find it harder to pay attention to you and stay awake!

Use some of the passion that you have for your subject to inject some feeling and natural emotion into your presentation. Keep the tone of your voice conversational. Think about the last chat you had with your best friend and talk just like that. Imagine having a conversation with each member of your audience.

> 📖 *See also:*
>
> *"Tip 101: Express your passion, enthusiasm and energy", page 58*
> *"Tip 68: Use a conversational style of talking", page 41*
> *"Tip 109: Slides should not be the focus of your presentation", page 62*

Tip 95: Lower the pitch of your voice	Intermediate

Psychologists will tell you that you have a better chance of getting your message accepted if you speak in a lower voice as this is perceived as being more authoritative.

Therefore, try to speak in the lowest tone of voice (the deepest pitch) that you can achieve whilst still talking comfortably. This can be especially important for women. Speak from the centre of your abdomen, not from your throat.

| Tip 96: Vary the speed of delivery | Intermediate |

As with the tone of the voice, the speed of our speaking is constantly changing during normal conversation. The number of words per minute increases and decreases depending on how excited we are, how important the subject matter is, and whether we want to focus on certain points or skim over others.

If you are reading out a pre-written speech and you talk at a constant speed during your presentation, it does not appear normal or natural and your audience will struggle to connect with you. You will sound like a machine. They will not be at ease while listening to what you are trying to say.

| Tip 97: Speak loudly, clearly and slowly | Essential |

It is surprising how many otherwise talented speakers, under the pressure of nerves and anxiety, stand up in front of an audience and consumed by their own insecurities and fears of inadequacy, are able to only quietly mumble through their presentation in such an ineffectual manner that it is highly unlikely that your audience will be able to hear their presentation, let alone accept their message!

The same nerves may also cause an inexperienced speaker to speak so fast that the audience cannot really absorb what is being said.

Do not let your nerves ruin your presentation. Speak loudly, clearly and slowly so that your audience can feel that you are confident and sure about what you are trying to tell them.

Rushing through your presentation to finish it quickly can make you difficult to understand. Articulate each word carefully and deliberately, especially if at times you feel you are going too fast.

| Tip 98: Use vocal special effects | Intermediate |

There are two effective vocal "special effects" you can use to vary the tone and pace of your presentation, and keep your audience on board.

Firstly, repeat key phrases that you want to emphasise and that you want your audience to remember.

Secondly, take a few-second pause before or after saying something important.

<u>*Example*</u>   "12 million people die every year from 'poor sanitation and unclean water.'"

<pause → eye contact → pause → eye contact → pause>

<repeat>

"Yes, 12 million people die every year from 'poor sanitation and unclean water.'"

<pause → eye contact → pause → eye contact → pause>

"That's same as the entire population of Belgium."

<pause → eye contact → pause → eye contact → pause>

"As if that wasn't enough, 3 million more die from air pollution. That's more than the population of Paris."

Tip 99: Be less technical	Essential

When you are creating your presentation, always ask yourself how technical you really need to be. An oral presentation is not going to be as effective or efficient as a written report in conveying technical facts. So if you want to convey raw data or lots of detailed information, consider pushing that material out of your presentation and into a handout or a document you can email out to your audience. Alternatively, offer to meet personally afterwards with those who are interested in the nitty gritty details.

Use your presentation to draw out the key conclusions or take-home messages, and invite the audience to find the extra detail elsewhere.

Suppose you are a specialist speaking to generalists or specialists in another field. Does your audience really need all the details? You should pay attention to this especially when you are presenting your own research or work, where it's easy to get carried away.

Tip 100: Don't denigrate the competition	Essential

Never use your privileged role as a public speaker to denigrate your competition. Your audience is doing you a favour by allowing you to be in the public arena. Do not abuse their trust by using your position to gain an unfair advantage over your competition.

If anything, try to be courteous and polite towards your competition, and you will find that your audience will respect you more for doing so.

Tip 101: Express your passion, enthusiasm and energy	Intermediate

If you want to convince your audience of your message, you will have to be convinced about it yourself, and allow your conviction to come across in your presentation. If your message doesn't matter to you, why should it matter to them? If it matters deeply to you, it will matter to them too. The presentation will not be convincing if the speaker does not exhibit conviction.

> You need to demonstrate total commitment to the problem, project, idea or outcome.

Be natural about it, and show your passion for your topic. Take the opportunity to literally tell your audience from the heart why you think this topic is vitally important. Even if you hate the topic, you can talk passionately about why you hate it so much.

State your case clearly, authentically and offer the strongest support for it. Be the strongest advocate for your point of view. Your audience can then choose to agree or disagree based on the merits of your argument.

It's fun to listen to someone who is truly into what they're discussing. Your audience will appreciate your honestly and openness. So don't hold back: be passionate and confident. Let your passion for your topic come out for all to see. Deliver the presentation with feeling, emotion, and energy. Deliver the presentation as if you have spent your entire life waiting for that moment.

Your enthusiasm will make you memorable. The twinkle in your eye, the tone of your voice, and your body movements should suggest excitement and interest. It will rub off on your audience. You'll see them sit up in their chairs and start really paying attention.

Tip 102: Think about body language	Intermediate

You ought to develop your own and unique style of body language which you feel comfortable with. Body language is a natural feature of human to human interaction and conveys non-verbal information which augments the spoken word. Adding body language to your presentation style can help you to animate your presentations in a natural way which will help build a connection and rapport with your audience.

You should practice your body language before the presentation to make sure you are giving the right signals at the right time. Generally you should aim to have an "open" body language, but in any case, your body language should reflect and reinforce your spoken comments.

Tip 103: Use audiovisual aids	Intermediate

Even if your presentation does not depend on slides or OHP transparencies, it is useful to have at least one such presentation aid, even if it is simply to give an outline of your presentation. It often makes the presentation more interesting and is appreciated by audiences.

Tip 104: Use attention grabbers	Intermediate

Remember that your audience can concentrate for approximately 15 minutes before attention starts to wander. Stand back from your presentation for a moment and think about whether you can incorporate attention grabbers at 10 or 15 minute intervals.

An attention grabber is something that will make your audience sit up and take notice of what you are saying. Use your imagination and the existing format of your presentation to come up with a novel way of injecting some life into your presentation and your audience. Typically, do something that will change the pace, or change the focus of your presentation. Maybe ask a provocative question or ask for some audience participation.

📖 *See also:*

"Tip 36: Open big", page 28

Tip 105: Use quotes that support your argument	Intermediate

One of the benefits of using pre-prepared slides in your presentation is the ability to introduce your audience to quotes from experts and display them on a large projector screen. This often has a compelling impact. Using a quote is a potent way of adding credibility to what you are saying.

You can present all the evidence you have to make your case convincing, but sometimes the thing that clinches the deal is a timely quote from an external authority that your audience respects and trusts. You can make a controversial statement more plausible and palatable by supporting it with a quote. That can make a difference between your audience accepting your claim or rejecting it.

📖 *See also:*

"Tip 49: Use quotations", page 33

Tip 106: Don't try to impress	Essential

Your motivation for your presentation should not be to impress your audience. You will not impress them by trying hard to impress them!

Instead, your genuine motivation should be to share, to help, to inspire, to teach, to inform, to guide, to persuade, or to motivate. If you succeed in doing these things, then almost certainly your audience will be both impressed and grateful at the same time.

See your presentation as an opportunity to serve your audience, not to impress or "sell" them.

📖 *See also:*

"Tip 74: Give them something", page 44

Tip 107: Make it sound impromptu	Intermediate

Although you will have prepared your talk to the last detail and rehearsed it until you can present it without any prompts or notes, you should aim to speak as though you are giving an impromptu talk – something that is natural, spontaneous, unrehearsed – something that is performed with little or no preparation.

This makes for a more natural delivery and your audience will appreciate what they will perceive as being a truly unique, once-in-a-lifetime performance.

Chapter 3: Preparing effective PowerPoint® slides

"If your words or images are not on point,
making them dance in color won't make them relevant."
– Edward Rolfe Tufte (1942-), American academic

The title of this chapter refers to Microsoft Office PowerPoint because this is the presentation program which 90% of readers will be familiar with. The tips in this chapter however are equally applicable to all presentation programs, such as Apple's Keynote and OpenOffice.org's Impress.

This chapter does not cover basic information about how to use these programs, as there are already a plethora of books and resources on the internet which address this. Rather, this chapter will be dedicated to tips which may help you make more effective use of these presentation programs in your presentations.

Tip 108: Know when to not use slides	Essential

There are certain situations when you should not use slides:

- **When you want your audience's undivided attention.** Using slides divides your audience's attention between you and the projector screen. It also conditions your audience to see you as someone who wants primarily to convey information such an instructor or a trainer, rather than as a leader who wants to command the audience's full attention.

- **When you want to build a personal relationship with your audience.** In some presentations your primary goal is to connect with your audience. Think of a candidate addressing a political rally or a CEO addressing the workforce. You want to look your audience in the eye and to convey a personal message to each individual member of your audience.

- **When you want your audience's participation.** The moment you start a presentation using slides, your audience can psychologically switch off, because they know that your presentation will be following a pre-determined and relatively fixed course. You have already set the content, scope, direction, and sequence of your presentation and the audience's role has been defined as passive observers.

| **Tip 109: Slides should not be the focus of your presentation** | Essential |

Your audience has come to see you, listen to you, interact with you, be moved by you and your message, and gain something from you. The focus of this encounter with your audience is you.

➢ Slides are a tool for you to get your message across to your audience.

The slides are the visual aids that complement and support your spoken word. The slides are not the reason that people have congregated. They have come to see you. You are the "star of the show", not your slides!

Your slides should be appropriate, memorable and helpful for your audience. Make sure that they do not distract or confuse your audience, or allow your audience to lose rapport with you. Slides should be an aid to communication, not a substitute for it.

| **Tip 110: Don't depend on slides** | Advanced |

Your presentation should not depend on your slides. Your speech should be able to stand on its own. Your slides may certainly help convey your message, but you should never be so reliant on your slides that you cannot communicate without referring to them as a crutch.

➢ The best presentations are given by those who never rely on their slides and who rarely look at them.

| **Tip 111: Plan your presentation before creating slides** | Essential |

Do not waste your time in creating slides before you have a clear vision of what you want to achieve with them, and what role they will play in your presentation.

First, decide what you want your audience to do as a result of experiencing your presentation. Then figure out what they need to know, in order to do what you want them to do. Then create a simple outline that logically and clearly develops your main points. Finally, create slides to support your message.

| **Tip 112: Ignore 90% of PowerPoint's functions** | Essential |

Presentation programs have developed to such an extent that most speakers can easily ignore 90% of their functions. You want to spend your time preparing the content, the delivery, the handout, and the interaction with your audience. You do not want to spend most of your time on the computer playing with toys.

Use simple or few transitions and animations. Limit your slides to a few words, and some high quality graphics. Learn how to insert video or audio clips, but only if your presentation would benefit from it. Apart from that, you can ignore most other functions.

Tip 113: The size of your slide set is irrelevant	Intermediate

People often ask me how many slides they should put into their presentations. The rule of thumb seems to be to have one slide for every minute of the presentation. For example, 30 slides for a 30 minute presentation. However, I don't like this attitude.

➢ Having a "1-minute per slide" rule is really not helpful.

In fact, it limits creativity and results in monotonous presentations that all progress at the industry-standard rate of 1-slide-per-minute!

You should not even think about how many slides are in your presentation. The question is what you do with each slide, not for how long it is up on the projector screen.

I have seen a speaker using 2 slides for a 1-hour presentation. I have someone using 10 slides for a 1-hour presentation. I have even seen someone using almost 300 slides for a 45-minute presentation! All of these were fantastic, top-notch presentations.

Typically, some slides will be used for several minutes while others (such as those with graphics, pictures or cartoons) can be flashed by in a few seconds to illustrate your point. Both of these strategies are perfectly acceptable. Your slides support your talk. Use as many or as few as you need to make your point.

Your audience and you should not even be conscious of how many slides have been used. You cannot dictate how long to spend on each slide. What matters is not how many slides you have, but what use you put them to and how they integrate with the rest of your presentation, and with your spoken word in particular.

Tip 114: Personalise the slides for each audience	Intermediate

If you are giving the same presentation for several different events or audiences, it is tempting to simply use the same slide set for every event. It is tempting to just pick up the file from your hard disk and take it with you to the event. However, personalizing the presentation for the unique time, place and audience can be a very effective technique as it shows respect for the uniqueness of the audience. Each audience feels it's unique, even if your message is the same across several presentations.

A simple way to personalise your slides is to add the event and venue details to the title slide at the beginning of the presentation. This takes only seconds and can be done just before you leave for the presentation. It is within the technical abilities of most speakers.

One slide set, but two different opening slides. Each set is now personalised for two different audiences

Tip 115: Have only one concept per slide	Intermediate

It may help you to organise your presentation if you plan your slides in such a way that each slide is used to convey only one concept or idea. This will also help your audience naturally follow the flow of your presentation.

If you find that there are several concepts being conveyed on one single slide, it often adds to clarity if you split one complex slide broken down into several simpler ones.

◁ There are too many ideas on this slide. The audience cannot absorb this much information from one slide.

It would be far better to split the slide into several smaller ones

Traditional slide: Too many concepts

New slide 1

New slide 2

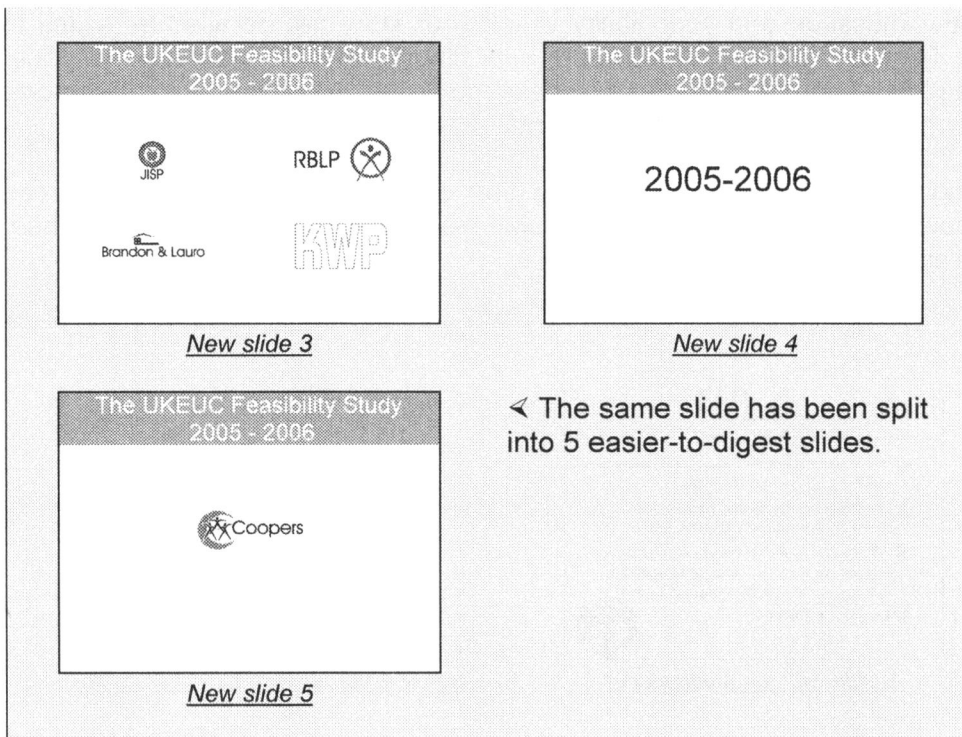

New slide 3

New slide 4

◁ The same slide has been split into 5 easier-to-digest slides.

New slide 5

Tip 116: What is the point of this slide?	Essential

Your slides should convey your points concisely, precisely and crisply. Whenever you make a slide, always ask yourself "What is the point that is being made with this slide?"

If the answer is not perfectly clear, you may want to re-phrase your text, or split the slide into two or more slides which are smaller, or find a graphic which would convey the point better.

Tip 117: Use simple slides	Essential

PowerPoint's features are sometimes used as a crutch by speakers who are afraid of communicating. Those who have little of substance to say, those who have presentations that are boring or irrelevant, and those who are afraid that their arguments are not convincing will see slide decorations and flashy animations and transitions as ways to distract from the fact that there are problems with their content.

Do not make your audience think this about you, and do not try to hide the inadequacy of your presentation by hyping up the packaging!

Your slides should be visually uncluttered. The less clutter you have on your slide, the more powerful your visual message will become. The fewer distractions you have the better. Usually you will have a hard enough time convincing your audience of your message. The last thing you want is for anything to get in the way of your message.

Don't let your message and your ability to tell your story get derailed by slides that are unnecessarily complicated, busy or full of superfluous decoration. Have the discipline to ask yourself "What does this add to my message?" and "How does this help promote my message or mission?" and "Are any elements in this slide non-essential?"

If something does not help you, then be firm and remove it from your presentation. Stripping down as much as you can often will make a huge, refreshing difference. Keep your slides clean, simple and efficient.

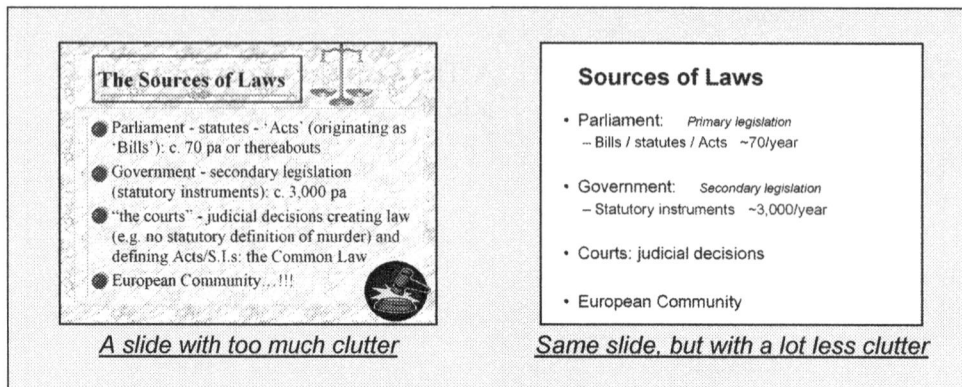

The Sources of Laws	Sources of Laws
A slide with too much clutter	*Same slide, but with a lot less clutter*

Tip 118: Limit the amount of text on your slides | Essential

Your audience cannot both listen to you *and* read your slides at the same time. Therefore, you should not show too much text on your slides. You will find that the best presenters hardly use text at all in their slides. It is useful to push technical, complicated or textual data into a handout.

When you do write text on your slides, do not write out everything that you will say! Use text to write down a simple, brief statement that can serve as a summary or introduction to what you will talk about. The text must not tell the complete story – otherwise your audience would be better served if you simply emailed them your presentation. The slides should not be like subtitles on the TV – they should not be a text version of what is already coming out of your mouth.

Slides should be used to support your presentation. They should not be able to stand on their own. They should not serve any purpose outside of the context of your live presentation. Presentation slides are ephemeral – something unique to that moment in time. Once your presentation is over, the purpose of your slides' existence is over.

The best slides may have no text at all. This may sound crazy given the dependency of text slides today, but the best slides will be virtually meaningless with out the narration that you provide. Remember, the slides are meant to support the narration of the speaker, not make the speaker superfluous.

If after my presentation someone ever asks me to email them a copy of my slides, I find this to be a great tragedy. Because it means that the person will be able to understand my slides from my presentation alone, which raises the question of whether I really needed to be there at all, and whether my presence actually added anything to the audience's experience.

➢ If your audience can understand your presentation from your slides, do you need to be there?

LITERARY READINGS

• **The Purpose**
By associating literature with the topics of economics, students from other disciplines experience an alternative way of representing and understanding economic ideas. This will enhance their understanding of economics as well as stimulate in them an appreciation of the beauty and meaning of literature.

Why South Africa?

South Africa is the country on the very Southern tip of Africa. I chose to do South Africa because when I was doing another project I discovered how amazingly high the HIV/AIDS category was and decided that it would contribute to society if people knew the effects.
So many people don't know what HIV/AIDS is or don't know how they can get it.
I took a survey and my question was:
HIV/AIDS is a disease that causes deaths; orphans, widowers, and widows; adult prevalence; people living with HIV/AIDS; and others. Which of these do you think is most important to help prevent?
30 people were surveyed and the results are to the right.

Text-heavy slides

◁ These slides have too much text.

The speakers will literally read the slide aloud. Their audiences will be forced to divide their attention between listening to the speakers and reading the slides.

Do these speakers need to actually be present?

"What is the purpose
of literary readings?"

Why did I
choose
South Africa?

Much better slides

◁ These slides serve as an aide-memoir and allows the speaker to talk and connect naturally with the audience.

The speaker will have to give the narrative orally rather than forcing the audience to read out his slides and listen to him reading them aloud for them!

📖 *See also:*

"Chapter 4: Preparing a handout", page 93
"Tip 99: Be less technical", page 5758

Tip 119: Avoid bullet points	Intermediate

When you create a new PowerPoint slide, you will notice that PowerPoint defaults to creating a slide with bullet points. As a result of this setting, many presenters and their audiences have come to believe that a good standard presentation would consist of bullet points. It has become the norm, and audiences have come to expect that your presentation would have bullet points.

However, bullet points are intended for lists. So unless you are showing a list of items – such as a shopping list, or a list of components, or a list of tasks – it is not natural or appropriate to display your presentation with a bullet list.

You are giving your presentation for the benefit of your audience. But from the audience's point of view, being presented with a list of factual statements can be a boring experience.

Although reading out a list of bullet points makes your presentation easy for you and makes your job a lot easier, from your audience's point of view, it makes your presentation feel formal, rigid and stiff. Believe me, you do not make it easier for your audience to love you if you subject them to an afternoon of bullet points.

So rather than spending your presentation talking around the bullet points on your slides, why don't you try alternative strategies such as giving your presentation in the form of a story. Design your slides to be used smoothly and simply to enhance and support your points as you tell the story. This can be done equally for technical presentations as for business presentations.

➢ Reserve bullet points for when you want to display lists.

Although many speakers will find this advice counter-intuitive and alien, I assure you that it is a tremendously liberating experience and a powerful way to shift the focus of your audience's attention away from the slides and onto you, the speaker, which makes for a far stronger connection between you and your audience. You will not be disappointed with the results!

#4 Teacher Study Groups in Schools
- Impetus = Teachers with some common interest or need
- Incentives = Collaboration, support from administration for a.r.
- Structure = Study group meetings, co-facilitation, on-going sharing of data commonly agreed upon – 'using the group'
- Outcome = Collective action, common next steps with students, on-going planning
- Audience = each other and peers outside group
- Leadership = Study group teacher members

Slide with bullet points

◁ There are bullet points on this slide, even though the presenter did not intend to show a list. Bullet points should be used only if you want to show a list.

Tip 120: Use blank slides	Advanced

To occasionally have a completely blank slide is an effective way to break the monotony of slides. This can be used to signal a natural break between sections of your presentation. Also, if you want to emphasise a particular point, making your projector screen go completely blank is a potent way to make your audience's attention shift away from the screen and onto you and what you are saying.

Also, after a couple of minutes of having a blank screen, your graphics in the following slides will appear all the more striking and will have greater impact.

Maybe you want to show a killer chart or graphic that will really sell your point... why don't you have a blank slide immediately before it and use the blank slide to look into the eyes of each member of your audience while you create a build-up and atmosphere for your key graphic. Then when you finally do show your graphic your audience will be so much more receptive to it and I expect you will be amazed with the result.

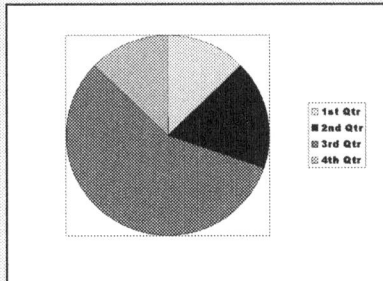

Slide 1

◁ In this presentation, the bar chart in slide 2 is shown immediately after the pie chart in slide 1.

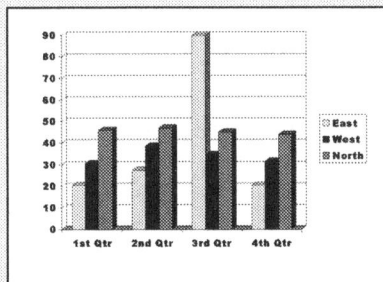

Slide 2

Slide 1

Slide 2

Slide 3

◁ In this presentation, there is a blank slide in between the two charts, so that the speaker can talk about the data before showing the bar chart (slide 3). This enhances the visual impact of the bar chart.

It does take confidence to include blank slides in a presentation. The thought of allowing the screen to become completely empty is scaring as all eyes are now on you!

Tip 121: Avoid using pre-designed templates	Intermediate

PowerPoint comes with a set of built-in design templates which you can use as the basis of the design of your slide set. Also, there are a lot more which can be downloaded from the internet, which are available free or for purchase.

While templates are invaluable for quickly adding a uniform design to your slides, I would only recommend their use by speakers who are absolute beginners at giving presentations. Even in such cases, it is debatable as to whether your time could be better spent practicing and perfecting any of the other aspects of presentation, than in selecting the perfect design template for your slides.

There are three key reasons for avoiding templates that other people have designed.

Back in 1990 when PowerPoint started to become famous, no one had seen the built-in design templates before and their use had the novelty factor and the cool factor. But nowadays, everyone is pretty bored of these templates and when you use them, they make you look old-fashioned.

A more important reason is that when you use a pre-designed template you lose the opportunity to exercise your creativity in making your slides. By taking an off-the-shelf solution you have missed out on the chance to make your own individual stamp on your slides. You want your audience to remember you, your presentation and your slides long after the event. A good way to do this is to design a set of slides that are memorable and distinctive, not anonymous and mass-produced.

Thirdly, many of the available templates are too distracting. They have too much clutter. As we discussed before, you should try to remove all clutter from your slides.

◁ The mountain background really does not add any value to this slide. It also diverts the audience's attention away from the chart, which is the main focus of the slide.

Is the template really needed?

Slide with pre-designed template

Tip 122: Use high-quality photos	Advanced

You should use the best quality (high resolution) photos in your presentations. You should never simply stretch a small, low-resolution photo to make it fit your layout as this degrade the resolution even further and the photo will appear very coarse and granular on the projection screen.

You can take your own high-quality photos with your own camera, or you can purchase professional stock photography on the internet. These are some of the websites where you can get high quality stock photos for use in your presentations:

http://www.istockphoto.com
http://www.sxc.hu
http://www.bigstockphoto.com
http://www.stockxpert.com
http://www.shutterstock.com
http://pro.corbis.com
http://www.flickr.com
http://www.123rf.com
http://creative.gettyimages.com
http://www.studio25.ro
http://www.morguefile.com
http://www.everystockphoto.com
http://www.fotolia.co.uk
http://www.stockvault.net
http://www.inmagine.com

http://www.freepixels.com
http://www.dreamstime.com
http://office.microsoft.com/en-gb/clipart
http://pdphoto.org
http://www.photocase.com
http://www.deviantart.com
http://www.freedigitalphotos.net
http://www.freephotosbank.com
http://nix.nasa.gov
http://www.geekphilosopher.com
http://www.freeimages.co.uk
http://www.freefoto.com
http://www.amazingtextures.com
http://www.freephotostation.com
http://yotophoto.com

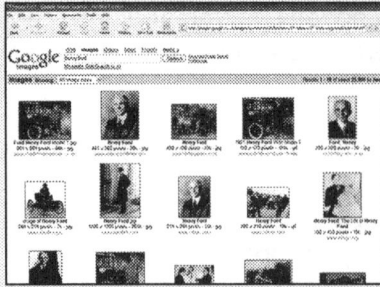
Screenshot from http://images.google.com

< A search on http://images.google.com will often return useful image results, although you must check the copyright and royalty status of any images you use.

Image of Henry Ford

http://www.wikipedia.org has an encyclopaedia-like entry on a vast array of topics and subjects in multiple languages.

Many entries have photographs and diagrams which have been released into the public domain and are available for general use.

< For example, this 1919 photo of Henry Ford is available from a link at http://en.wikipedia.org/wiki/Ford

Tip 123: Use photos instead of text	Advanced

Slides are best employed as a visual and graphic illustrative aid, not as a document that your audience is expected to read. One of the best uses of slides in a presentation is to convey graphical messages and information.

➤ Pictures, graphs and other images are especially helpful as humans are visual creatures.

The old adage that a picture is worth a thousand words is especially true in the context of a talk. Photographs in particular can be incredibly powerful in silently conveying a (subconscious) message through the projector screen while you are talking, and if used properly can greatly magnify the impact of your presentation.

How many photos should you use? How often should you use a photo?

I will answer this question with another question: "Why use words when you can say the same thing with a picture?" The simple answer therefore is that you should use photos as often as you can.

A text-heavy slide

◁ The traditional slide with lots of bullet points. The speaker would read out aloud the bullet points and tend to speak what is already written on the slide.

Does the speaker actually need to be at this presentation? Or can he simply email the presentation to the audience? What does the speaker add to this presentation?

An alternative approach is to use photos instead of text.

This presentation is better able to hold the attention and interest of the audience. ⱴ

Slide 1

◁ "...Those of you who have been at Bellevue Hospital for a while will know that we used to have a real problem with how our junior doctors were supported during their early stages of their professional lives. The juniors were unhappy with their work, and their supervisors were not satisfied with their performance. This is why 3 years ago we set up a mentoring programme for our junior doctors. And at the outset we had 4 hopes and aspirations for this programme..."

Slide 2

◁ "... Firstly, we wanted all our junior doctors to grow and develop during these early formative years of their careers..."

Slide 3

◁ "... Secondly, we wanted them to enjoy their work. We wanted them to come to work happy, and gain some satisfaction from the jobs they did, and go home wanting to come back again the next day..."

Slide 4

◁ "... Thirdly, we wanted our junior doctors to feel part of the community at Bellevue. We wanted them to be strong team players who would be reliable, dependable and committed to their work here."

You can see that removing the text from the slides and replacing it with photos has freed the speaker from the rigid confines of the bullet points. He no longer has to read out the bullet points from the screen and is able to look the audience in the eyes and talk to them in a more conversational, human and natural manner.

This makes your presentation much more powerful and memorable.

Tip 124: Adapt the photos to your context | Advanced

If you have sufficient proficiency with graphics software such as Photoshop or PaintshopPro, you should modify the photos to suit the exact situation that you are talking about.

For example, you may want to make a composite picture from several sources or add some text such as a quotation.

The original photo

◁ Photo of the Houses of Parliament, from Wikipedia. The photo can be adapted to any number of uses.

"If you like laws and sausages, you should never watch either one being made!"
– Otto von Bismarck
Chancellor of the German Empire between 1871 and 1890

The final slide

◁ Adobe Photoshop has been used to remove the cloudy sky from the background and to crop out the River Thames. This gives the building itself more attention. A relevant quotation has been added.

Tip 125: Use living photos	Advanced

When you use photos in your slides, your slides will have a greater impact if you have photos of living things and humans in particular. So for example, have photos of people, faces, animals, your family or your colleagues.

This creates an emotional link between your presentation and your audience and helps lodge your points in their brains.

IFS

Child poverty: why did it fall? And why didn't it fall far enough?

Bruce Jenkins
Institute for Fiscal Strategy
12th March 2007

Original title slide: boring

◁ The original title slide is functional but boring and sterile.

Child poverty: why did it fall? And why didn't it fall far enough?

Bruce Jenkins
Institute for Fiscal Strategy

12th March 2007

Slide with striking graphics

◁ The same slide with human imagery which complements the title itself brings the entire slide to life.

The audience naturally connects with the two children and becomes interested in hearing the speaker tell their story.

Tip 126: Fill the screen with your focus of interest	Intermediate

When you project a photo or other image during a presentation, fill up the slide as much as possible. In the example below the same graphic has a completely different impact and effect because it fills the frame. When speaking in public, don't underestimate the impact potential of your visuals.

75

Dementia

• 20% of people over 80 have dementia

Original slide

◁ The photo of the man is a peripheral item in the original slide.

20% of people over 80 have dementia

Slide focusing on area of interest

◁ In this slide, the man is immediately the main focus of the slide.

The audience can connect with the human face and the slide has much greater impact.

After connecting with the human face, the natural reaction is to be curious about the statistic and engage with the narrative of the slide.

Tip 127: Personalise the slides with unique photos	Advanced

If you are going to a larger event with multiple speakers such as a conference, a more challenging yet rewarding technique is to use your digital camera to take photos that your audience can relate with, download them onto your laptop or a computer at the venue, and incorporate them into your presentation.

Examples of memorable things to include are conference venue, event organisers, programme, keynote speakers, the hotel's headed notepaper, hotel lobby, sponsors' goodies or even photos taken during your flight, train or road journey to the event.

This makes your audience feel that your slides were made purely for that event. It gives the impression that you have gone to great lengths to prepare for that particular presentation. Of course, you must make a natural reference to these things in the talk itself. Your audience will feel really honoured to be receiving a one of a kind, unique, special presentation tailored for that particular audience in that event at that particular time.

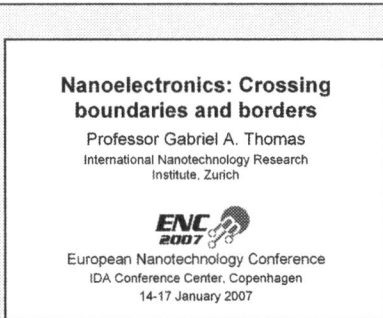

Nanoelectronics: Crossing boundaries and borders

Professor Gabriel A. Thomas

International Nanotechnology Research Institute, Zurich

ENC 2007

European Nanotechnology Conference
IDA Conference Center, Copenhagen
14-17 January 2007

Slide 1

◁ "Good morning, my name is Gabriel Thomas, I work at the International Nanotechnology Research Institute in Zurich..."

Slide 2

◁ "...Copenhagen is a great city and it's a tremendous pleasure for me to be here today in Denmark on the second day of the 2006 European Nanotechnology Conference..."

Slide 3

◁ "...Like many of you, my group and I almost didn't make it for the start of the conference yesterday because of air traffic delays getting in to Copenhagen... it seemed like the whole world was trying to come to our conference this year...!"

Slide 4

◁ "... Each year we have more and more delegates coming to this conference, and it's always really nice to catch up with old friends and hopefully make some new ones too..."

Slide 5

◁ "...I would like start by thanking Professor Frederiksen and his team for all their hard work in putting together an absolutely fantastic conference this year, and for making all of us feel so welcome.

"The title of my talk today is 'Nanoelectronics: Crossing boundaries and borders'..."

⋀ It is easy to take some photos with a digital camera and incorporate them into your slides. These are photos of the airport, the aircraft that the speaker travelled in, the conference hall and the conference organising committee: these photos could only have been taken at the conference itself!

Your audience will appreciate that these slides were designed and created purely and exclusively for this conference, this meeting, this audience. These slides are unique for this event and will not be used ever again.

This is an incredibly powerful way to connect with your audience and give a highly personalised presentation.

Tip 128: Avoid clip art	Intermediate

Clip art used to be in fashion in the 1990's and PowerPoint includes a range of commonly-used clip art. When clip art became popular, access to high quality photos in digital form was very limited: this was of course before the days of digital cameras and inexpensive scanners!

Today, access to digital cameras, scanners and stock photo websites on the internet (see "Tip 122: Use high-quality photos", page 71) is so widespread that the use of clip art in a presentation does seem old-fashioned and amateurish.

Even if you yourself have limited access to such technology, you can almost certainly ask a friend, colleague or relative who will be able to help you create your presentation with high quality photos rather than clip art.

Original slide with clip art

◁ The original slide has clip art to depict a school bus.

Slide with photo

This slide has a photo of a school bus and conveys the same imagery but in a much more vivid and striking way. It makes for a slide which holds more appeal for the audience.

Tip 129: Use photos or cartoons for humour	Advanced

Photos which are humorous in themselves, or if you can provide a humorous anecdote, story or caption are a great way to provide some light relief in an otherwise heavy presentation. They give the audience the chance to switch off for a few moments and recharge for the slides which follow.

The same effect can be achieved with cartoon, either with captions or with captions that you provide live.

As with all humour and jokes in particular, timing is paramount. You must therefore practice the delivery of such slides beforehand until you get the timing right and can perform them smoothly and naturally.

Tip 130: Build a library of wildcard photo slides	Advanced

As you give more and more presentations you will soon accumulate a collection of generic photos and slides. These can form your library of wildcard slides which you can drop into any future presentations. This will save time as you will not have to reinvent the wheel for each presentation.

Often there is no intrinsic meaning to these slides. You must use your imagination to build a story or anecdote (real or fictional) surrounding the slide which you can tailor to the presentation you are giving and the audience you are presenting to, in order to reinforce the point you want to make.

A wildcard slide – taking camels to the local camel market in the back of a pickup truck

◁ I took this photo while on holiday a few years ago and then made it into a slide.

As a slide, it has absolutely no meaning on its own. It can therefore be used in a wide variety of different presentations.

Simply add your own story, anecdote, joke, case or example.

Tip 131: Be careful about hidden meanings in images	Intermediate

When you are selecting your photos for your slides, be aware that there may be cultural and gender differences in the way certain imagery is interpreted. Your images may be perceived by others as having an implied meaning which you did not envisage.

This is particularly a concern if you will be presenting to an international or a foreign audience.

Tip 132: Don't go overboard with PowerPoint	Essential

Unless your presentation is specifically about demonstrating how to use PowerPoint, it should not be used to showing off your mastery of PowerPoint. There is a time and place for that, and an important presentation is not the time or place for gimmickry.

It is preferable to have simple and elegant slides. It is better to err on the side of simplicity when designing your slides than risking your audience being distracted by the vehicle of your message.

Tip 133: Use transitions and animations sparingly	Essential

PowerPoint's fades, transitions, backgrounds, sound effects, and so on can be a real pitfall for presenters. Firstly, you can waste a lot of time preparing glitzy presentations – time which could be better invested in research, planning and rehearsal.

Secondly, they can give your audience the impression that you care more about surface than about substance.

However, there are certain situations where careful and sparing use of PowerPoint's animations and transitions can be used to really good effect:

- When your presentation has been heavy and serious for a while and you want to lighten the mood.

- When you want to change the pace of the presentation.

- When you want to signal the start of a new part of your presentation.

- When you want to build a diagram.

📖 *See also:*

"Tip 142: Use object builds", page 8558

Tip 134: Keep charts simple	Essential

Presenters often put too much data in their slides, without thinking about exactly what they want to say by showing that data. There is usually no need to show all your data in the form of a chart during your presentation. You need to be selective and decide which data to show.

First decide what point you want to make and what message you want to give to your audience. Based on that, select out the data that will support you, and decide on the best way to display it. You can always give your audience your full data set in a handout.

Tip 135: Use a sensible font	Essential

The fonts that you choose for your text can say something about you, your personality, your message and your professionalism. Your choice of fonts can communicate subtle messages to your audience, and so you should choose fonts deliberately.

➢ If your objective is to convey professionalism, do not use fancy fonts such as Papyrus or Comic Sans.

You should bear in mind that people at the back of the room also need to be able to see your text, so make the font size big enough.

Closing Thoughts

- The Earth is getting warmer
- Human activity may not be the main cause
- Global warming may not be a bad thing
- Technological solutions may be available and relatively simple

Original slide with script font

◁ The selection of font in the original slide damages the presenter's ability to deliver a serious message.

Closing Thoughts

- The Earth is getting warmer
- Human activity may not be the main cause
- Global warming may not be a bad thing
- Technological solutions may be available and relatively simple

Same slide with a more formal font (Arial)

Tip 136: Limit the number of fonts	Essential

Do not go overboard and choose a whole bunch of different fonts. Be consistent throughout your presentation and at most, use one or two fonts.

Each font or style should be used consistently throughout your presentation as it will help your audience understand meaning through your use of style.

Tip 137: Serif or sans serif?	Essential

Fonts can be classified as being either serif fonts or sans serif fonts.

Serif fonts such as Times New Roman have structural details on the end of strokes that make up letters and symbols. These are easier to read in printed materials.

San-serif fonts such as Arial and Helvetica are better for reading materials on computer monitors and projector screens.

The Quick Brown Fox Jumps Over The Lazy Dog.

ABCDEFGHIJKLMNOPQRSTUVWXYZ
abcdefghijklmnopqrstuvwxyz 0123456789

A The Adobe Garamond Pro typeface, an example of a serif font

Helvetica:
The Quick Brown Fox Jumps Over The Lazy Dog.

A The Helvetica typeface, an example of a serif font

Tip 138: Take the font with you	Intermediate

You may have a corporate font or a favourite font that you want to use in your presentation. Be aware that the set of fonts that are installed on the computer where you made your presentation may not be same set of fonts on the computer where your presentation will ultimately be shown.

If the destination computer does not have the same font installed, you may face a range of issues depending on how exactly the font information was stored in your presentation and the software settings on the two computers.

For example, the computer may try to find the most closely matched font and substitute that for your font, although this process may distort the layout of your slides. Alternatively the destination computer may designate your presentation file as being "read only" and you will be unable to make any last-minute changes to your presentation at the venue.

To avoid such problems, use only those fonts that are installed as standard with your computer, unless you are prepared and able to take the font package with you and install it on the computer where you will be showing your presentation.

Tip 139: Use colour	Intermediate

You should give a thought to using colour in your presentation. You can apply colour to the slide background, the text and the graphic elements.

➤ Colour is an important non-verbal communication tool.

You can convey a lot of meaning simply through a careful selection of colour. Also, colour evokes feelings and emotions. The right colour can help motivate and persuade. There is evidence that the use of colour can increase interest and improve understanding and retention of information.

For example, red can be used to reinforce your message to your audience that they must not do a particular thing; green can be used to indicate that a course of action is safe and should proceed. Cool backgrounds such as blue and green can help an audience relax, while warm backgrounds such as orange and red can stimulate the audience.

Make sure that your choice of colours is complementary and contrasting, although never clashing. Avoid using too many different colours, and keep the colour scheme simple, consistent and easy to understand.

Finally, remember that upto 10% of the population has some difficulty with colour perception, so don't rely on colour alone for distinguishing meaning between different types of text.

Tip 140: Select backgrounds carefully	Intermediate

As a general rule, your slides' background should match the ambient light in the room where you will be giving the presentation.

So, if you are presenting in a brightly lit seminar room, you should keep the lights on and use a light background; if you are presenting in a large, dim lecture theatre, use a dark background.

There should be good contrast between the background and the text. If your slide background is light, your text should be dark; if your slide background is dark, your text should be light.

Tip 141: Include a presentation progress tracker	Essential

No matter how well your presentation is progressing, your audience will want to know for how much longer you will be speaking.

If you are using slides or OHP transparencies it is an easy matter to let your audience know at the start how many slides or transparencies you will be showing, and then to number each one. This also helps you make sure they are in the correct sequential order before you start your presentation!

Another way is to have a "progress indicator" incorporated into your slides as in the examples below.

Introduction
- Lorem ipsum dolor sit amet, consectetuer adipiscing elit.
- Vivamus aliquet interdum enim.
- Fusce viverra neque quis dui.
- Quisque vehicula dictum metus.
- Phasellus consectetuer lectus eget quam molestie laoreet.

Introduction ···· • Background ···· • New horizons ···· • Future goals

Slide 1

Background
- In auctor lacinia odio.
- Suspendisse viverra lectus et neque.
- Etiam adipiscing pede ut dolor euismod semper.
- Vivamus sagittis dui ut dui.
- Mauris viverra aliquet erat.

Introduction ···· • Background ···· • New horizons ···· • Future goals

Slide 2

Each slide has a "progress indicator" at the very bottom, so that the audience has a way of knowing whereabouts in the presentation they are.

New horizons
- Nulla nec metus ac enim gravida dignissim.
- Aenean et velit sit amet nibh scelerisque lacinia.
- Integer aliquet consectetuer dui.

Introduction ···· • Background ···· • New horizons ···· • Future goals

Slide 3

Future goals
- Sed vulputate metus quis nisi.
- Donec quis leo in lorem aliquam tempor.
- Vivamus vel quam vel urna ornare condimentum.
- Duis interdum ante non lectus.

Introduction ···· • Background ···· • New horizons ···· • Future goals

Slide 4

📖 *See also:*

"Tip 45: Give your audience a way of tracking progress", page 32

Tip 142: Use object builds	Advanced

Object builds (also called animations), if used judiciously, can have a stunning impact on your presentation.

Object builds such as bullet points, should not be used on every slide. Some animation is a good thing, but stick to the most subtle and professional ones.

➢ The real power of animations lies in their use to build an argument or draw a diagram.

Slide 1 — Vroom's Expectancy Theory 1964: EFFORT

Slide 2 — Vroom's Expectancy Theory 1964: EFFORT ....→1ST LEVEL OUTCOMES

Slide 3 — Vroom's Expectancy Theory 1964: EFFORT ....→1ST LEVEL OUTCOMES ....→ 2ND LEVEL OUTCOMES

Slide 4 — Vroom's Expectancy Theory 1964: EFFORT ....→1ST LEVEL OUTCOMES ....→ 2ND LEVEL OUTCOMES — EXPECTANCY

Slide 5 — Vroom's Expectancy Theory 1964: EFFORT ....→1ST LEVEL OUTCOMES ....→ 2ND LEVEL OUTCOMES — EXPECTANCY, INSTRUMENTALITY

Slide 6 — Vroom's Expectancy Theory 1964: EFFORT ....→1ST LEVEL OUTCOMES ....→ 2ND LEVEL OUTCOMES — VALENCE, EXPECTANCY, INSTRUMENTALITY

↖ A complex diagram is built sequentially using custom animation.

With each mouse click, another part of the diagram is shown. The speaker can spend as much time is required on each section of the diagram, before clicking the mouse to reveal the next part.

The more complex the diagram, the more effective this technique can be.

📖 *See also:*

   "Tip 82: Draw a diagram", page 49

Tip 143: Avoid sound effects	Essential

PowerPoint comes with a set of audio clips which you can use in your presentations. However, you should generally avoid using them because the use of superfluous sound effects is a sure way to lose credibility with your audience.

📖 *See also:*

   "Tip 128: Avoid clip art", page 78

Tip 144: Use video or audio	Advanced

Although you should avoid the use of stock audio clips, the situation is completely different in the case of video and audio files which should be used in your presentation when appropriate.

Using video or audio to show concrete examples to illustrate your point is an effective way to communicate with your audience. It also serves as a change of pace thereby increasing the interest of your audience.

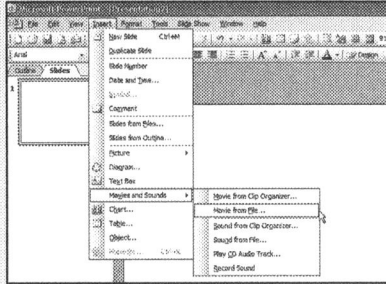

Step 1: Insert menu > Movies and sound > Movie from File

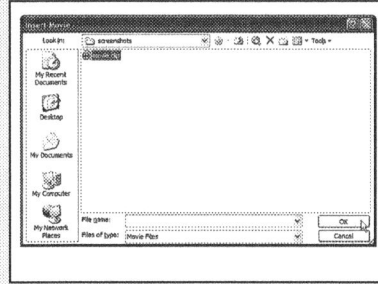

Step 2: Select your MP3 or WAV file

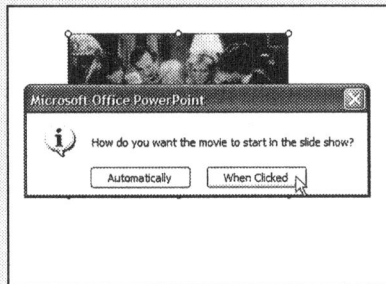

Step 3: Select whether the clip will play automatically or when you click the image

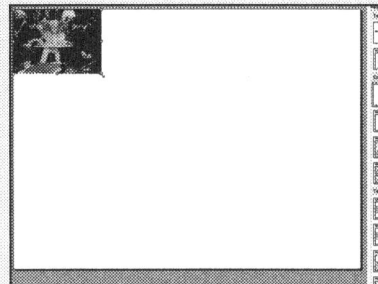

Step 4: Position the thumbnail image at the top-left corner of the slide

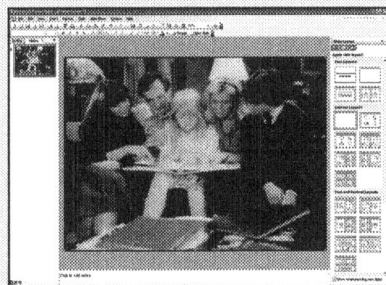

Step 5: Resize the thumbnail to fill the whole slide

↗ It is easy to insert audio and movie clips into your presentations.

Make sure that all sound and movie files are located in the same folder as the presentation that you've created, and that you insert them from this location. Sound and movie files, because of their large size, don't become an actual part of the presentation file – a link is formed to the file. When the presentation is played, the program looks for the sound at the location described in the link.

This works fine on the original machine where the slides were created, but as soon as you move things to another machine, if the links don't accurately describe where the files are, things fail to play. PowerPoint will always look for the sound in the folder that contains the presentation, so this is the best place to put them.

Tip 145: Use declarations in your titles	Intermediate

Write the titles of your slides using declarative sentences.

A declarative sentence (or declaration) makes a statement such as "I am going home." Your title will read more like a headline rather than just a title or category and this can help make your point more forcibly.

Tip 146: Vary the text, graphics and audio	Essential

No matter how interesting your presentation is and no matter how slick your presentation style is, you will soon bore and tire your audience if you subject them to an end endless barrage of text slides. The same applies to a long chain of graphic-heavy slides which demand a lot of thought and mental processing activity from your audience.

You should avoid this tedium by having some variety in the sequence of your slides. After a short run of text slides, insert some photos, and after some photos, return to text or some audio or video. You can maintain your audience's interest and attention in this way.

Tip 147: Don't put logos on every slide	Intermediate

It is a good idea to put your name and title on your first slide, but avoid putting them as headers on all the slides. Similarly, avoid putting your corporate logo on every slide because this can distract from the message of your talk.

If you do have to have a logo because of corporate policy, place it discretely as a watermark so it does not get in the way.

Tip 148: Simple rules for text slides	Essential

If you must use textual slides, there are some general rules:

- Maximum 7 lines in height
- Maximum 7 words in width
- Maximum 5 words in title

➤ If you find that you need more space, consider splitting your slide into smaller ones.

Remember that slides should only be used as an aide-memoir for the speaker and the audience – the audience should not spend their time reading slides!

Tip 149: Avoid text effects	Essential

Text effects such as drop shadows may be fine for written material, but they look out of place in presentations. They may detract from your message.

You should also avoid typing all the text of your presentation in CAPITAL LETTERS as this makes it more difficult for your audience to read.

Tip 150: Simple rules for OHP transparencies	Essential

Although currently out of fashion, OHP transparencies can be a powerful tool for group activities such as brainstorming sessions. When you are giving your presentation with pre-prepared OHP transparencies, however, follow these rules:

- Maximum 10 lines in height
- Maximum 7 words in width
- Maximum 5 words in title

Effective and smooth use of OHP transparencies does need some practice so that you can place them appropriately and change them with minimum fuss and without disrupting the flow of your presentation or your audience's concentration.

Tip 151: Make some notes for yourself	Essential

If you would like some notes as an aide-memoir when you are presenting, you may find it PowerPoint's "print handout" feature helpful. It will print out miniature versions of your slides. You can then annotate them and add any brief notes that may help you.

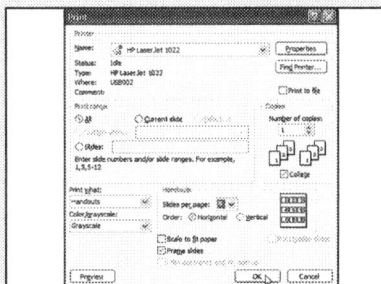

◁ On the print options page, select "Handouts" and the number of slides to show per sheet of paper.

Screenshot of print page

Print out of handout page

◁ You will get a print out with thumbnails of your slides. This can be annotated with brief notes for each slide, for your own benefit as an aide-memoir and prompt during your presentation.

📖 *See also:*

"Tip 88: Don't use a written script", page 52

Tip 152: Accept white space	Intermediate

Do not feel compelled to fill empty areas on your slide with your logo or other unnecessary graphics or text boxes that do not contribute to better understanding.

Slide with white space

Be comfortable with white space. This slide has only two words. The speaker's job is to give the presentation, not read loud the slides.

Nothing further is needed on this slide.

Tip 153: Include an end slide	Intermediate

It is more satisfying for your audience when you have an end slide. A slide that makes it clear that it is the last and final slide.

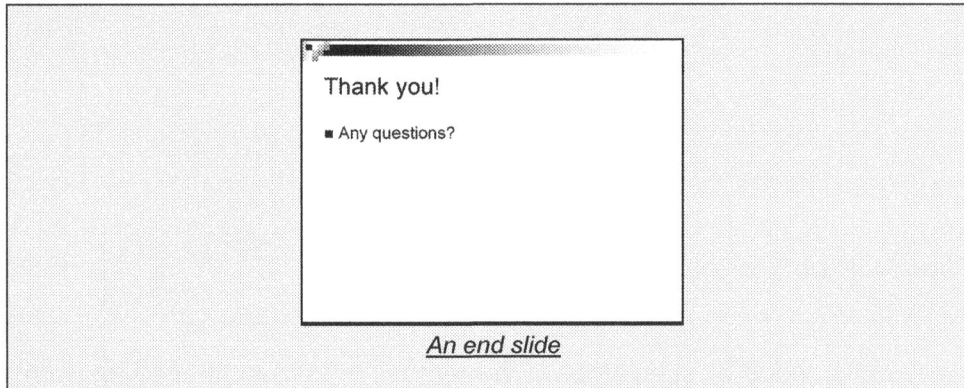

Thank you!

■ Any questions?

An end slide

📖 *See also:*

"Tip 57: Have a definite termination", page 37

Tip 154: Make it big enough	Essential

Whenever you use any form of visual aid such as slides or props, make sure that they are big enough and positioned so that everyone in the room can see it clearly. For smaller items you may need to pass them around the room so that everyone can see them.

Tip 155: Use the slide sorter	Intermediate

Even though you will have planned the logical flow of your presentation, it sometimes helps to view the final slide set in slide sorter view where you can get a bird's eye overview of your presentation.

With the slide sorter view it is usually a simple matter to change the order of the slides or even move whole sections around.

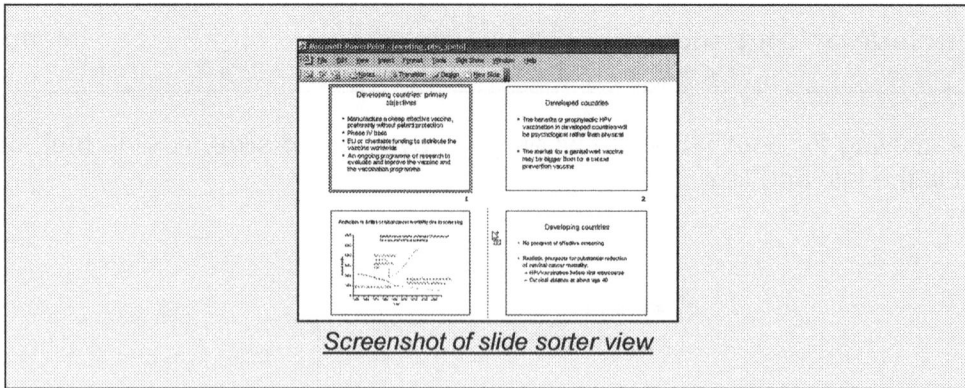

Screenshot of slide sorter view

Tip 156: Take all the pieces with you	Essential

If you've used audio, video or special fonts, remember to take all those files with you as well as your presentation. They are not saved with the PowerPoint file itself.

Chapter 4: Preparing a handout

"The greatest gift is to give people your enlightenment, to share it. It has to be the greatest."
– Siddhartha Gautama (circa 563BCE-483BCE), founder of Buddhism

So, you have created your presentation, congratulations! That's a big task over and done with. But hang on... how about making a handout?

➢ A handout is a very useful thing to distribute at your presentation.

Audiences are much better served receiving a detailed, written handout which highlights your content from the presentation and expands on that content, than a mere copy of your slides. If you have a detailed handout or publication for the audience to be passed out after your talk, you need not feel compelled to fill your slides with a great deal of text.

Tip 157: Make a high quality handout	Intermediate

The design and quality of the handout reflects on you, your approach to the subject, and your attitudes towards your audience. The technology is available for you to provide your audience with constantly up-to-date, high quality, effective handouts which can have a number of uses:

- A handout can reiterate your message.

- You can give your audience supporting data / graphs / charts from your presentation.

- You can give your audience a summary of the main points.

- You can give your audience a reading list.

- A handout helps your audience remember your message long after the presentation is over.

- If your presentation is running behind schedule, you can miss out certain sections if they are covered in your handout.

- A handout provides your audience with a way to contact you in the future.

- You can reinforce your credibility and professionalism with a well-designed handout.

- Your message can reach people who were not at the presentation if you give out a good handout.

The information density of the handout can be very high. A large amount of information can be included, particularly if you give consideration to the way you design the handout.

Tip 158: Audiences expect a handout	Intermediate

Modern audiences have come to *expect* to take home a handout of some sort, whether it's:

- A printed handout
- A CD-ROM / DVD of your slides or supporting files
- Or at least your website's URL where they can download files and material from.

Handouts are an integral part of most technical presentations these days, and their design, use and distribution require careful planning.

Tip 159: Choose the best time to distribute your handout	Advanced

You can distribute your handout before, during, or after your presentation, depending on what you want to achieve with your handout, and what role it plays in your presentation. You audience will probably look at your handout right when they receive it and will miss whatever you say in the next several minutes.

Handouts given before presentations

At times it can be very useful to give your audience a handout several days before your presentation. Typically, this would apply in situations such as:

- If the members of you audience had levels of background knowledge and you wanted to bring all of them up to speed at a particular level before they attended your presentation. Then when you started your presentation, you may assume a basic common foundation level of knowledge and spend your precious presentation time building on that rather than spending it giving background information.

- If you wanted your audience to do some essential background reading before your presentation, you could give them a handout based around a reading list. Your presentation could then be focused around that common reading.

- When you wanted to give your audience some exercises or questions to do before they attend your presentation, so that you can spend some time during your presentation discussing their responses to those exercises.

- If you wanted to invite audience interaction on your data, results or proposal, it helps to circulate a handout well in advance of your presentation so that your audience will come having considered your ideas and will be in a more considered position to engage in a constructive dialogue during your presentation.

There are a number of pitfalls to watch out for with this strategy, however. If you have given a comprehensive handout beforehand, then your audience may respond in the following way:

- They may not read it before they attend, in which case your time, effort and energy have been wasted.

- They may spend the time during the presentation reading your handout rather than focusing on you.

- They may feel that they received all the information they needed, and therefore do not need to attend.

- They may lose interest in your topic and therefore not attend.

Handouts given during presentations

Making your audience interact with your handout during the presentation is an incredibly powerful way to involve the audience in your presentation. When the audience has put something of themselves into a handout, they may value it more than an anonymous piece of printed paper that someone has simply given them.

There are several good ways of achieving this:

- Handouts with gaps. Give out a skeleton handout at the beginning with headings and broad topic areas and lots of white space so that your audience can fill in their own notes under each heading during the presentation. This type of handout pre-structures the session and acts as an advance organiser. It helps keep your audience on track with the flow of your presentation.

- If you want to show a complex table or chart of data, and feel that not everyone at the back of the room will be able to see the whole data, a handout containing the table or data is an ideal supplementary aid. It may help to involve the audience in labelling or annotating the data under your guidance as a way of engaging your audience.

- Interactive handouts and worksheets. These include tasks and exercises for audience members to perform during the lecture, either individually or in pairs or in groups, with space on the handout for them to write down their ideas and responses. The answers can be a basis for further discussion.

It can be a logistical challenge to distribute handouts to a large audience without causing a disruption to the flow of the presentation, so it is worthwhile thinking about how you will distribute your handout. If you let your audience have the handout at the beginning of the presentation, it may act as a distraction.

If you have a large amount of content, consider breaking it up into a number of smaller handouts that you can distribute at appropriate times during your presentation. This prevents your audience from reading ahead and losing interest in what you're saying.

Handouts given after presentations

If you want your audience to go away from your presentation with a summary of your presentation, you should make the handout available only after you have finished your talk.

There can be considerable difficulty in deciding what to tell your audience during the presentation about the handout that will be available afterwards. If you tell them about the handout at the start of the presentation, they may not take any notes, expecting your handout to be more comprehensive than it is.

If however you distribute a handout at the end of the presentation without announcing that you were intending to do so, this can be interpreted as a vote of no confidence in the audience's note-taking abilities, and some of them may feel cheated because they took notes unnecessarily.

The further challenge is that if people generally know that you distribute comprehensive handouts after your presentation, they may simply ask a colleague to pick up a copy for them, rather than attending your presentation at all!

Tip 160: Plan handouts while planning your talk	Intermediate

Your handouts will be a reflection of your presentation, so you should plan them at the same time as the talk itself. In order to make handouts that are complementary to your presentation, you need to make them when you are in the same mindset as you are when you are planning your presentation.

Do not rush the process of making handouts. Bear in mind that your audience will remember you and your presentation for years to come, on the basis of this handout. So it is worthwhile investing some time and thought into the planning of your handout.

Tip 161: Do not simply give a printout of your slides	Intermediate

Slides are a one-to-many way of communication, while handouts are one-to-one. The style you use in writing your slides is really not the most suitable style for writing your presentation.

You cannot go in depth on a slide. But with a written handout you can go as deep as you want to or need to.

Also, many slides include bullet lists. A list of bullet points when read two days later will be confusing for your reader. They will not remember the context of the bullet points after the event.

Tip 162: Write a separate document	Intermediate

The best handouts are written as a separate document altogether. Start with a blank slate and write down what you want to convey to your audience. Do not take a shortcut by simply giving a copy of your slides or notes.

Tip 163: Link your handout to your presentation	Intermediate

When your audience looks at your handout after the presentation, the handout should jog their memories about the presentation itself. The handout should serve as a reminder of their interaction with you.

A good way of doing this is to include thumbnails of your key slides to link your handout to the presentation. In effect, you will be giving your audience an annotated version of your slides.

Tip 164: Make it obvious what it is	Essential

Days, week, months, even years after your presentation, you want your audience to look at your handout and remember your presentation. Therefore, include as much detail as possible about their meeting with you:

- Title of presentation
- Date and time of presentation
- Venue
- Who the audience was

Tip 165: Outline your presentation	Essential

A good starting point for your handout is the outline of your aims and objectives for your presentation. Include the key take-home messages, keywords and concepts that you wanted to impart to your audience.

You should include the structure of the presentation, using the same headings and sub-headings to show the relative importance of points as you did in your slides or speech.

Tip 166: Give your contact information	Essential

In order that your audience may contact you later on, make sure you have included your comprehensive contact information:

- Your name
- Your title and organization
- Phone numbers
- Business address
- E-mail address
- Website

Tip 167: Let them get more copies	Intermediate

You will be surprised how a popular handout can become widely distributed. It may fall into the hands of people who did not even attend the event!

It is helpful if you have a way to allow people to get more copies of the handout. Uploading it to a website or having the materials ready to email out to interested people is an easy and effective way of increasing the reach and lifespan of your handout.

Make sure you include this information on your handout so that people can download or ask you for their own copy of the handout.

Tip 168: Use sensible formatting	Essential

Your handout should be easy to read. Have a margin of at least 2 cm on every side and use serif fonts such as Times New Roman) which are more distinctive to read in print than sans serif fonts such as Arial are.

Leave plenty of white space for people to annotate their own notes. It is usually preferable to print the handout on only one side of the paper, leaving the reverse side for annotation and notes.

📖 *See also:*

"Tip 137: Serif or sans serif?", page 82

Tip 169: Use a clear writing style	Essential

Use a clear, simple style of writing. Avoid jargon unless absolutely necessary. Think about each point you want to convey to your reader, and say it in the most concise way possible. Once you have made your point, do not waffle.

Re-read your handout and remove any unnecessary words and phrases which do not add anything to the message you want to convey.

Tip 170: Have an action plan	Intermediate

Be clear as to what you want your audience to achieve as a result of your presentation, whether it is change their working practices, or become aware of an issue, or learn a new skill.

Include your recommended practical action plan in your handout.

> See also:
>
> *"Tip 56: Have a call to action", page 36*

Tip 171: Make your handout appealing to the eye	Advanced

Handouts should be attractive, easy to read, and comprehensive. Avoid using starbursts, ornate borders, or too many fonts or styles. Set off distinct parts of the handout using italics, shading, bold, or underlining.

Illustrations and graphics can make your handout more reader friendly.

Tip 172: Don't let the handout distract your audience	Essential

People concentrate on one line of thought at a time. If you give them something to read during your presentation that doesn't match the content and style of your talk, they will cut themselves off from one in order to follow another.

Tip 173: Make it the right length	Essential

The length of the handouts should match the length and complexity of the presentation. A short presentation of 10 to 15 minutes may require only one or two pages of handout material. Longer presentations of an hour or more may call for four to six pages or more of handout material.

If your handout is too short it will be seen as derisory; if it is too long your audience will disengage and switch off.

Tip 174: Have a reading list	Advanced

Including a list of recommended reading, references or website URLs is a good use of a handout. Consider annotating them the reading list to highlight the relative importance and benefit of each item and to indicate functional alternatives where possible.

Tip 175: Include supporting materials	Intermediate

The handout is an ideal place to present supporting evidence for claims you make during your presentation. Include in your handout the charts, graphs, data, tables etc. that are not suitable for showing in slides.

Tip 176: Make the handout stand alone	Advanced

Whereas the slide set should not be able to stand alone, the situation is reversed in the case of your handout. Your handout should be able to stand alone as an independent document.

➢ When your audience refers to your handout a month after the presentation, will the answers they need be at their fingertips?

Tip 177: Make the handout in good time	Essential

Design and print the handout well ahead of time to avoid problems such as running out of paper and photocopiers breaking down.

Tip 178: Keep your handout updated	Intermediate

It is a good idea to keep your handouts updated regularly.

This will save you a lot of time the next time you give the same or similar presentation. Another benefit is that if someone asks for another copy of the handout in the meantime, you do not have to worry about whether it is still accurate or relevant.

Consider keeping all your handouts in the same folder in your computer to help you locate it quickly.

Chapter 5: Rehearsals

"The harder I practice, the luckier I get."
– Gary Player (1935-), South African professional golfer

Tip 179: Practice, practice, practice	Essential

After you have spent time researching your presentation, writing it and perfected the slides, you must now practice and rehearse your presentation until you can deliver it perfectly, fluently and naturally.

When you go to buy an expensive suit would you ever dream of buying it without trying in on first? No, of course not! The same is true with your presentation. Don't expect your audience to wear it before you have tried it on for size yourself.

The worst case scenario is that the first time you give the presentation is when you are in front of a live audience.

When you get there, you want to know in the back of your mind that you have already given that same presentation at least 100 times. Won't that give you some confidence?

There are no shortcuts to this process. You need to practice giving your presentation to the point that you can do it half awake with a blindfold on and no slides or props.

Tip 180: Use the practice to perfect the presentation	Essential

It is amazing how you often I think that I have created a perfectly reasoned, argued and presented presentation on paper, but it is only when I stand up to practice it, and I say the words I am planning to say, and look at the slides I am intending to show... that I realise that there are big problems with my presentation and that a lot more work is required!

Your presentation may seem reasonable on paper, but you will find out what works and what doesn't work in real life only by performing it time and time again.

When you are doing a dry-run of your presentation you will inevitably get flashes of inspiration which compel you revisit certain sections and re-design them for the better. You should also become more relaxed and identify redundant or problematic sections in your presentation which may need more work (which *may* involve more basic research).

During this stage of the preparation, you also need to keep a look out for the following:

- Slides that don't make the point as strongly and as naturally as you had hoped
- Slides that just don't work well in that sequence
- Slides that don't flow well together.

When you practice, you should imagine that you are performing it at the venue in front of your intended audience.

Tip 181: Be comfortable when you practice	Essential

You should aim to be comfortable when you practice as this will allow you to get the most out of your practice session.

Practice in a place where you will be fully comfortable. Don't practice when you're too tired, hungry, preoccupied or distracted to derive any benefit from it. Switch off the TV, radio and your mobile phone. Avoid places where you might be overlooked or overheard as that will make you self-conscious.

Practicing is a creative process and you will need to draw on your imagination and creativity to find better ways of saying what you want to say.

Tip 182: Find a human audience	Intermediate

After you have practiced your presentation to such an extent that you are completely happy with it, the next step is to subject yourself to a human audience!

This could be your spouse or partner, a work colleague, or even your boss. You must ask them to give you truthful and constructive feedback on your performance. You should find someone who has sufficient time, interest and a relationship with you such that they can give you brutally honest feedback. You want them to rip you apart so that you can put yourself together again and make it better in the process.

You should note all comments with sincerity – there is no point in arguing with them or telling them how they are wrong. Doing so will only alienate the very people who can help you give a better presentation.

Simply make a note (either mental or on paper) of all their points and thank them for that. Then it is down to you to analyse whether their comments have any weight, whether they are correct or appropriate, and whether you have scope for implementing their suggestions.

Tip 183: Have a dress rehearsal	Essential

When you are satisfied that your preparation is almost complete, and you have rehearsed it enough times to make you comfortable about delivering it, you should have at least one dress rehearsal in front of a real audience. During this session, ask your audience not to interrupt, but the save their comments until the end. As part of these staged rehearsals, you should also practice taking questions from your audience.

Tip 184: Make the presentation look effortless	Advanced

You will know when you have practiced and perfected your presentation – when you have done the best you can – when you are able to make your presentation look easy, even if the actual material is difficult. This stage comes with practice, and your confidence will be boosted tremendously when you have reached this level of preparedness.

Tip 185: Accept the 80-90% rule	Essential

No matter how much you practice your presentation, when the day comes you will only be able to deliver 80-90% of your ability. The same is true for professional athletes and sportspersons. The pressure, time constraints, public view, and a variety of other reasons cause you to be less than perfect.

What this means is that (1) your best ever performance will actually occur in private when no-one is watching and (2) you need to practice such that in practice sessions you are performing at 110-120% of your best performance!

Tip 186: Pay attention to your time allocation	Essential

When you design your presentation, you must plan its length in accordance with the time allocation you have been given. In fact, you should aim to finish your presentation a few minutes short of your time allocation.

If your presentation is a lot shorter than what was asked of you, the event organiser or session chairperson will have to find a way of filling in the gap that you have created in the programme. If you run over your time allocation you risk alienating your audience, the person who has asked you to speak, or those who will be speaking after you.

In a conference situation it is better to be a little short than to be cut off by the bell. Make your points short and snappy: nothing kills a good conference presentation like rambling.

Tip 187: Make landmarks for timing	Intermediate

During your rehearsals make a note at what time you reach certain points in your presentation. If you know where should be at a given time, you can use a watch during your presentation to keep track of how fast you are progressing through your presentation.

If you are ahead of schedule, you are going too fast and losing people. If you are behind schedule, leave out some material rather than going over time.

Tip 188: Rehearse the Q&A	Intermediate

When you are rehearsing your presentation, you should also think about the worst possible questions, and rehearse your answers out loud. If your human audience is not sufficiently technically aware to think of questions (such as your spouse), you should write out some questions for them to ask you.

Tip 189: Videotape yourself	Advanced

The most realistic way to get feedback about your presentation style, delivery and impact is to videotape yourself whilst you are practising or actually performing your presentation. In some ways, this is a far superior way to get honest feedback than asking a human audience who may feel inhibited by out of politeness or affection.

➢ The video never lies.

This can be a very scary process of self-discovery, but you will definitely learn a lot about how you communicate, your facial expressions, body language and mannerisms.

Also, there are certain things which you may not like about your presentation style which would be very difficult for your audience to describe to you. This however is easy for you to detect if you could watch yourself performing your presentation.

If you do not have access to a suitable video camera, you might want to try the "record" function of your computer's webcam, a dictaphone or at the very least a mirror!

Tip 190: Use a spell checker	Intermediate

Spelling mistakes are not acceptable. Your audience will fixate on them and may even laugh at you. They will not pay attention to what you're saying.

➢ Run your slides and handout through a spell-checker.

Spell-checkers are not perfect as they cannot detect if you have used the wrong word – they can only detect that you have spelt it incorrectly.

Therefore, make sure you proofread everything yourself, and then ask a friend or colleague to proofread for you - they will pick up things that you did not notice.

Chapter 6: Just before the presentation

"Before everything else, getting ready is the secret to success."
– Henry Ford (1863–1947), American industrialist

So your big day has finally arrived! All the hours of preparation are behind you, and you can now get down to concentrating on the serious fun of delivering your presentation.

This may sound far-fetched, but if you have diligently done your homework, it is quite feasible that by the morning of the presentation you will actually be really charged up and raring to get out there and deliver it. You will be confident because you have seriously researched your topic, you have prepared your presentation, and you have rehearsed it until you can say it in your sleep and even if your script gets lost. You will ready for success. You will be unstoppable!

Tip 191: Arrive in town early	Essential

There is still a lot of preparatory work to be done in the final hours before your presentation. This preparation is vital for your success. So if you are travelling a long distance for your presentation, you should aim to arrive at the destination city well in advance of the time of your presentation, preferably the previous day.

Tip 192: Get local information	Intermediate

The day before your presentation you must get some local information. This will help you relate to your audience better and can provide useful conversation starters. You can also incorporate some local news or information into your presentation. This will make it more personalised for that audience. It will give an impression that you have created the talk especially for them, for that meeting, for that very event.

Find something personal or unique to the time, the place and the audience. Add what you learn into your speech or your slides to underscore the idea that the presentation, the location, and the audience are coming together to create a once-in-a-lifetime moment.

- Read the local paper
- Take a walk or drive around to connect with local people
- Get quotes, stories, and facts
- Take digital pictures of the venue / delegates to insert into presentations

Do this because you want to learn about your audience and what is important to them. You want to connect with them. Do it because you respect the uniqueness of the audience, the time, the place.

Tip 193: Get a good night's sleep	Essential

You should aim to have a restful night before the day of your presentation. The day of your presentation will no doubt be stressful and demanding and you can help yourself by having good quality rest and food the night before.

- Have a good meal
- No alcohol
- No partying
- Speak with your family
- Set your alarm to get up early
- Use 2 alarm clocks!
- Sleep early
- If you cannot sleep, spend some time rehearsing your presentation
- Have a good breakfast in the morning.

Tip 194: Scan the news	Advanced

On the day of the presentation you should make a final scan in the industry news sources to see if there is anything new relevant to your field of presentation. When you are presenting, you need to be the most up-to-date person in the room.

If you are at a different city, find an internet access point and use it to find out if there have been any new developments since you prepared your presentation. You must be aware of any breaking developments or announcements in your field, and you should be prepared to make last-minute changes to your presentation to incorporate these changes. You will gain immeasurable credibility in the eyes of your audience if you can do this comfortably.

Tip 195: Dress like a leader	Intermediate

You will hear contrasting advice regarding how you should dress when you give a presentation. Some advocate dressing better than your audience, while others advocate "dressing down." Others with recommend that you dress neutrally or that you wear whatever makes you feel comfortable.

What fuels this debate is that different types of dressing are appropriate for different settings, so didactically prescribing a one-size-fits-all mantra is not helpful.

I recommend a different approach: you should dress in such a way that your audience can accept you as a leader.

By adopting this approach, you are placing the emphasis on what will make it easier for your audience to accept you and your message. The concept that different styles of dressing are appropriate in different settings is already implied within this approach.

As a caveat however, you should avoid wearing clothes that may distract your audience from your message. The focus of your presentation is to get your audience listening to what you're saying, not wondering about your dress sense.

Colours are a matter of personal style but as a general rule it is usually appropriate to dress in neural colours, if only to avoid people focusing on your daring and flamboyant dress sense rather than focusing on your message. The same applies for patterned colours which should be avoided, in favour of pastel colours.

Generally, you should make sure your clothes are clean and pressed and that your personal grooming is smart, clean and presentable.

They are the speaker who motivates the audience to admire and respect them. They know they have succeeded when people say, "I want to be like him (or her)."

Tip 196: Be there for the whole event	Advanced

If your conference spans several days and starts before the day of your presentation, try to attend the conference from the very beginning.

If you are scheduled to speak at a meeting at 8:15pm and the meeting starts at 7:00pm, arrive at 6:00pm.

Be ready to adapt your remarks depending on what you hear, see, and feel. Weave what goes on before your presentation into your own presentation. Refer by name to the speaker before you. Ask permission of an audience member to use his name in reference to your topic. This gives the impression that your presentation has been personalised for this unique audience.

Tip 197: Familiarise yourself with the venue room	Essential

When you visit the room where you will be delivering your presentation, you must use this opportunity to familiarise yourself with the room in as much intimate detail as possible.

You must identify the following:

- The podium
- Where the chairperson will be sitting
- Where your audience will be sitting
- The distance between the podium and the chairperson

- The distance between the podium and your audience
- Is the presenter expected to stand / sit at a particular position, or is there flexibility for the presenter to move around the room or stage?
- What are the acoustics of the room
- How your voice travels across the room, and how loud you must talk in order to be heard in all areas of the room
- How you will control your slide presentation
- Whether you have access to a pointer

Tip 198: Optimise the environment	Intermediate

Taking charge of the environment is part of your job as a speaker. It may sometimes be possible to optimise the venue to suit the style and format of your presentation, and to make sure the environment is conducive for a productive interaction between you and your audience.

Check that the heating, lighting, ventilation and equipment are satisfactory. Your audience will fall asleep if the room is too warm and stuffy. They will not be able to concentrate if the room is too cold. A dark room makes eye contact difficult. If the slide projector is not working, you need to arrange for a repair or replacement in good time!

Tip 199: Rearrange the furniture	Advanced

How you layout the seating arrangements can have a fundamental impact on the format and running of your presentation.

- Serried rows of chairs mean that the audience can see only the speaker. This restricts participation and suggests a more formal atmosphere.

- Circular or semi-circular arrangement of chairs or desks means that the audience can see each other, implying that everyone is expected to contribute.

- The presence of desks in a brightly lit room suggests that the audience should take notes during the presentation.

If you find the seating arrangement is not suited to the format of your presentation, then try to get the seating arrangement changed to the way you want it.

See also:

"Tip 30: Decide on the most appropriate format", page 24

Tip 200: Master the technology	Essential

You must master whichever technology you will use for your presentation:

✓ Back projection   ✓ Video   ✓ Laser pointer
✓ Microphone   ✓ Slide projector   ✓ Lighting circuit

If you cannot operate any of these items of equipment, it gives your audience the impression that you have not had the respect or decency to prepare properly for the talk. Nothing irritates an audience more than watching somebody fiddle with a computer after the start of a presentation.

Tip 201: Load your slides onto the venue's computer	Essential

When you arrive at the venue make it a priority to put your presentation onto the computer that will be running it.

Some events will require you to have submitted your presentation file several weeks in advance of the event. The file should then be already available for you to use on the day.

If you have brought your presentation files on a USB memory stick, floppy disk or CD-ROM, it is advisable to transfer your files from your media device onto the computer where it will be used rather than running the presentation from the media itself.

This eliminates the risk of any last-minute connectivity problems between your media and the computer. Further, computers are unable to read large files from media devices quickly, and so your presentation may run slowly with unpredictable pauses if you attempt to run a large presentation from a media device. Again, this problem is eliminated if you transfer your presentation onto the computer itself.

Alternatively you may be able to connect your own laptop computer to the venue's projector and run your presentation from your own laptop. If you are planning to do this, do make sure that the connecting cable is compatible and functioning and that you laptop battery is charged up.

The sooner you do this, the more time you and the event organisers have to correct any compatibility problems. You do not want to be in the situation where you are at the lectern to deliver your talk and are unable to access your presentation files due to a connectivity problem.

Tip 202: Preview your slides	Essential

After checking that you are able to transfer your presentation files onto the computer, you must take some time to preview your presentation in the actual room where you will be delivering it.

There are several different versions of operating systems and presentation software, so you want to make sure that your files are compatible with the venue's hardware and software. Even though you will have checked for compatibility beforehand, you can never be certain of compatibility until you reach the venue and preview your slides.

Further, the features of the room are difficult to predict beforehand. It may be that the edges of your slides are cut off when projected onto the screen or that your colour scheme becomes warped by the projector's brightness and contrast settings or the room's ambient lighting.

This is the only time you will have to make any last-minute changes to your presentation – there is still time to change fonts and colours or to add or remove slides. If you have taken some digital photos of the venue or city, now is your last chance to insert them into your presentation.

Finally, run through the presentation and make sure the slide transitions and animations are working as intended. If your presentation requires animation for the intended impact, it will be embarrassing if you find out during the presentation itself that the venue's computer does not handle the animation as you expected.

Tip 203: Remove all accessories	Essential

Let's face it: for most people, giving a presentation is going to be a stressful experience.

Giving a presentation is a performance. A show. An act. A drama. The presenter is on display to the whole world as he or she bares all to reveal himself or herself to the audience.

The last thing you, as the presenter, need at this difficult time is anything that is going to get in the way of you giving your best performance.

➤ You don't really want any distractions right now.

You want to remove from your environment any obstacles or dangers that are not strictly needed.

With this is mind, this is a list of things which you can safely leave behind on your desk or in your bag when you are called to the podium:

- **Mobile phone** – it *will* ring or vibrate at the most inopportune moment. Anyway, were you planning to call for a pizza in the middle of your presentation?

- **Watch** – it *will* jingle or beep

- **Pens** – the time for writing notes is long gone

- **Keys** – are you going to open doors during your presentation?

- **Coins** – you *will* put your hands in your pockets and jingle your keys

- **Credit cards** – they *will* fall out of your pockets if you have to bend over to pick something up

- **Sweets** – they *will* melt with your body heat

- **Chewing gum** – why have an obstruction in your mouth while you are trying to make your voice heard across the room? You risk unwittingly projecting it at high speed towards an innocent member of the audience

- **ID badge** – your audience already knows exactly who you are. Anyway, no one can read your badge from a distance.

- **Jewellery** – you *will* nervously fidget with rings, necklaces or earrings when you are struggling with awkward questions or if there is a problem during your presentation.

The focus of your presentation is your message, which is important, interesting, relevant and useful. Taking any of these things to the podium with you can allow them to distract from you and your message.

More importantly, these are all familiar personal items which people rely on as comforters in a stressful situation. Grow above and beyond such a childish attachment and leave them behind. They are not needed for your presentation, and your presentation should be the only thing you and your audience should be thinking about at this time.

Tip 204: Warm up your voice	Essential

Athletes and sportspersons will tell you that before a race or game it is vitally important for them to warm up thoroughly. It is not possible or advisable to launch straight into activity without warming up. The same is true of singers and theatre actors who will typically perform a set of voice exercises to warm up before a performance.

The same rule applies to you and your presentation.

You cannot expect to wake up in the morning and stumble into a presentation in front of a thousand listeners and expect your voice to naturally produce its best tones and melodies on demand. This is simply unrealistic.

When you arrive at the venue, identify a private spot where you will not be disturbed or embarrassed, and perform the following exercises:

- Yawn
- Rub your face
- Screw up your face, aiming to use every muscle in your mouth, face and neck
- Stretch and rotate your neck
- Stretch your arms and rotate your shoulders
- Stand on tiptoes or jump on the spot
- Bend forwards and touch your toes
- Open your mouth and say "Ah", starting at your lowest pitch and increasing the pitch to your highest
- Shout as loud as you can

You will need to use trial and error to develop a warm-up routine that suits you and which you are comfortable to carry out. It should only take a few minutes and the idea is to stimulate your body into action, rather than tire you out.

I can guarantee that after you have completed even a simple warm-up routine, you will feel a lot more in tune with the task that lies ahead of you.

Tip 205: Rehearse the presentation one last time	Essential

After you have loaded your slides, checked that they work, analysed the structure of the room and done your warm-up, now is the time for a final dress rehearsal.

Go to the room where you will be presenting, and with no one else in the room, stand at the podium, take a deep breath and practice your presentation one last time.

Use this opportunity to remind yourself about the sequence of your presentation, to figure out how loud you have to talk, to practice any demonstrations and get yourself mentally and psychologically ready.

At the end of this dress rehearsal, you can think of yourself as the pilot of an aircraft standing at the start of the runway. Your aircraft is fully fuelled for the journey. The engines have been warmed up. The flaps, ailerons and elevators have been tested. All the passengers are seated and their luggage is secured. You are waiting just for the control tower to give you permission to take off.

Tip 206: Be a host, not just another speaker	Advanced

Most presenters think of themselves as just speakers, whose role is to read a speech out loud to a group of people.

This is a bad approach. For the duration of your talk at least – and preferably for the duration of the entire session in which you are talking – you should think of yourself as a host at a dinner party, and your audience as being your invited guests.

As with a dinner party, the host's job is to make the event a pleasurable experience for the guests. The host has organised the event and is responsible for coordinating the event and making sure everything runs as planned. It is the host's job to make sure each guest is entertained and finds the event interesting, and to make sure all the needs of each guest are catered for.

The same applies to you, the speaker at a meeting or conference.

Do not view your audience as your enemies or adversaries. They are not there to cause you problems. Rather, they are your valued and loved guests. The event that you are the host of is none other than your presentation.

Tip 207: Meet your guests	Intermediate

As a consequence of the previous tip, before your talk, try to meet as many people as you can. Meet people. Talk to them. Let them make contact with you. Even if you only talk to a few people, others will get the feeling that you are an approachable, interesting and likeable person. If you talk with someone, talk about them instead of yourself.

Try not to spend more than 2-3 minutes with any one person; but bounce around and circulate with your audience. If your session is large, you may only get to say hello with 5-10 people, but these folks could be your supporters that you focus on during the session.

Then when you get on the podium, your audience will recognise you as someone they were talking it. And you will recognise them as your new-found friends. This is a good way to heighten your audience's concern for you.

This allows for a more natural conversation between the speaker and the listeners, as all the preliminary introductions and ice-breakers have already happened and you can talk to friends rather than talking to strangers.

Establish rapport with your audience, and they become your partners in a dialog, allies in your presentation. They'll want you to succeed. They'll overlook your nervousness and lack of polish. They'll laugh at jokes they've heard before. And they'll give you the benefit of the doubt even if they lose the thread of your logic.

Tip 208: Have a soft drink before you start	Essential

A dry mouth is a very common feature of the anxiety response that many people experience when they have to speak in public. When your mouth is dry, it makes it difficult for the tongue and lips to move properly when you speak. As a result you struggle to get the words out properly!

You can overcome this by taking small sips of water very frequently while you are waiting to be called to give your presentation. Don't drink so much that you need to visit the toilet every few minutes, but just enough to keep your mouth, tongue and lips wet. Make sure you swill the drink in your mouth for maximum effect.

Plain water is possibly the best drink for this purpose as it is usually readily available and won't damage your teeth when you swill it inside your mouth!

Tip 209: Take a drink to the lectern	Essential

You should do this only if it suits your style of presentation and if you think that you will have a dry throat during the presentation. In this case, having a drink available can be a real boon.

However, this does come with a price – it can be acutely embarrassing if you spill your drink whilst in the public gaze! So it is only probably worthwhile taking a drink with you if you will be speaking for a long time, or if there will be a break during your present

Tip 210: Go to the toilet before you start	Essential

You want to be comfortable when you are giving your presentation, so make sure you visit the toilet before you start your presentation. The last thing you need during your performance is to be distracted by a full bladder.

Chapter 7: Last-minute tips for confidence

"The Human Brain starts working the moment you are born
and never stops until you stand up to speak in public!"
– Sir George Jessel (1824-1883), English judge

So you have reached your event and you are about to go to the podium. You feel your pulse racing and your body trembling and you start panicking.

Hang on, you shouldn't even be panicking!

➤ If you have read and acted on the first part of this book, you will have done almost everything you can do to become a confident speaker:

- **You will have done all the preparation that is possible for this event.**
  See: "Chapter 1: Planning for your presentation", page 7

- **You will be an expert on your topic** - no one will know more about your topic or your presentation than you do. You know what you are talking about.
  See: "Tip 19: Research your topic thoroughly – be an expert", page 18

- **You will have something important, interesting, relevant and worthwhile to say** – your audience is eager to hear what you want to say and you owe it to them to give them what they need from you.
  See: "Tip 13: Have something important to say", page 16
  See: "Tip 14: Have something interesting to say", page 16
  See: "Tip 15: Have something relevant to say", page 16

- **You will have spent time on preparing your slides.** You will have taken the time to build the logical flow of your presentation, and designed supporting materials that are professional and appropriate.
  See: "Chapter 3: Preparing effective PowerPoint® slides", page 61
  See: "Tip 29: Have a logical, clear structure", page 23
  See: "Chapter 4: Preparing a handout", page 93

- **You will have rehearsed your presentation** so much that you can deliver it without really thinking about what you are saying or doing.
  See: "Chapter 5: Rehearsals", page 103

- **You will have actually reached the venue in good time!**
  See: "Tip 191: Arrive in town early", page 109

If you look at the tips in this book, 210 tips been covered so far, with only the final 63 remaining. Therefore, more than 75% of the work of giving a presentation lies in the preparation, with less than 25% of the work involving the actual presentation itself.

Now is the time to put all your anxieties, worries and stresses behind you. Focus now on the moment, secure and comforted by the knowledge that you are at the peak of Mount Everest. Things are going to be dead easy from now on.

So relax, compose yourself, and think only about doing what you have practised so many times in the past few days. And try to enjoy this experience.

Tip 211: It is normal to be anxious	Essential

Even experienced speakers get nervous. You should not be afraid of butterflies. They're a normal and healthy feeling. It means that your senses are heightened and you're ready to perform. Most public speakers have butterflies before starting a presentation.

➢ It is normal, natural and appropriate to have a degree of nervousness about the event, as that feeling of nerves will force you to give your best performance.

Instead of trying to eliminate your jitters, turn them into positive energy you can use to boost your delivery. Get rid of those chemical and psychological reactions by becoming message-centred and audience-centred, not self-centred.

Tip 212: Don't be self-centred	Intermediate

You should stop concentrating on yourself, but instead focus your attention away from your own anxieties and focus on your message and your audience.

Most stage fright is rooted in self-preoccupation – "How am I doing?", "Am I making any sense?", "Am I making a fool of myself?"

Stop focusing on yourself. Focus, instead, on your audience and on how your speech is going to help them. "How are you doing?", "Do you get this?", "Can you hear me?"

Be careful though – don't take out your stress on them. Don't ask them too often if they are OK as a way of shifting attention away from you.

Tip 213: Don't let nerves ruin your presentation	Essential

You have put so much into your presentation that the last thing you want is to have it destroyed by your own negative forces! What a waste of time and effort that would be. Don't be so nervous that you are paralysed because of your nerves. Use your nervousness and turn it into a positive energy.

Tip 214: They won't find you boring	Essential

If you're not boring in real life, there's no reason for you to be boring as a speaker.

Fear is the culprit. When you're afraid, you become self-protective. You draw back into yourself. Your focus narrows to what is immediately around you, and all you can think about is survival. You lose your creativity, spontaneity, and humour.

Control your nervousness, and your natural liveliness will surface.

Tip 215: Don't be afraid of laughter	Advanced

Many speakers have a fear that the audience won't take them seriously. There is a fear that your presentation will be met with ridicule and laughter.

➢ Relax. If you do or say something that amuses people, they will laugh -- even if you don't want them to.

So laugh with your audience. Then they're not laughing at you, they're laughing with you. And they'll love you for it.

Laughter is the most potent antidote to fear. While fear shuts you down and makes you cower in the corner, laughter pumps you up and gets you energized.

Tip 216: Release excess energy	Essential

Stress and nerves gear your body up for exercise. So exercise your body to control your stress and release the excess energy.

Arrive early at the venue and take a brisk walk for at least five minutes. If it is raining or snowing outside, you can still walk up and down the stairs.

For trembling hands, place your hands on the side of your chair, and count to ten as you try to lift the seat. Imagine yourself channelling all your energy into your hands, and then imagine all that energy flowing out of your hands into the chair like electricity being conducted away from you. This is an exercise you can do without anyone noticing you doing it.

Stand on one leg and shake the other. Now, switch sides. You want your energy to go through the floor and out of your head. Shake your hands...fast. Hold them above your head, bending at the wrist and elbow and then bring your hands back down.

Eat something that is rich in carbohydrates before the presentation. Something like a sandwich or some chocolate. Not only will it make you feel better but it will divert some of your excess energy to your stomach and intestines.

Simple exercises such as shrugging the shoulders or tensing and releasing your body are also helpful. Listening to music helps relieve pressure. Do whatever it takes to release some of the energy that accompanies anxiety.

Tip 217: Control your breathing	Intermediate

If your natural tendency is to pant in shallow breaths when you are nervous, you can control this by consciously forcing yourself to take slower, deeper breaths. This sends a signal to your brain that you have nothing to fear. It helps to calm you down.

Reduce your nervousness by taking several deep breaths immediately before you're introduced. In the thirty seconds before you begin speaking, take three slow, deep breaths through your nose, filling your belly. As you breathe out, say to yourself, "Relax."

Tip 218: Give yourself permission to fail	Advanced

Many speakers make their nerves even worse by having unrealistic expectations about their performance. They feel that they must deliver a perfect, flawless performance each and every time. This makes their nerves even worse, which further dampens their performance. A self-fulfilling prophecy is set up in this way, which is bound to end in disappointment.

You are a human being and so you should give yourself permission to not give the perfect presentation! Relax a little and don't punish yourself over your performance. Give yourself permission to make mistakes. No one is perfect in real life. All you can do is rely on the preparation you have made so far, relax and hope for the best.

You are only human and nobody is perfect. Your audience mostly won't notice your mistakes, as you are the only person who knows what you intend to say in your presentation, only you will notice if you deviate from this plan.

Furthermore, even an obvious mistake will seem much more important to you than it will to your audience. The best approach is just to carry on regardless, laughing it off if necessary. Think back to when you've seen others deal well with mistakes—what did they do?

Tip 219: Have rituals	Intermediate

Rituals can help you focus, get you into the same groove. Rituals can be anything, but as long as it takes you back to the familiar it's good, it's less frightening.

Tip 220: Don't apologise for nervousness	Intermediate

Research shows that most people report noticing little or no anxiety in a speaker, even if the speaker himself reports feeling a lot of anxiety. The point is that your audience probably will not notice your nerves even though you may think that it is obvious for all to see.

One way of helping yourself is to appear confident and calm. And in particular, don't go around telling everyone how nervous you really are or how you're not going to give a good presentation! Nothing kills an audience's positivism as much as the presenter telling people how bad he is.

Look confident, feel confident, be confident. This makes for a better presentation. Audiences hate arrogance and cockiness, but they love confidence, if it is genuine.

Most people won't see how nervous you are. They can't tell if your palms are sweating or your knees are knocking or your heart is pounding. So don't tell them.

Smile. Hold your chin up. Stick your chest out. Look confident, even if you don't feel it. After a while you'll begin to feel it too.

Tip 221: Think positive thoughts	Intermediate

Mentally put all your negative thoughts into one folder and press the "delete" button on all your negativity. Replace your negative thoughts with strong, positive, happy thoughts. Tell yourself that you're going to be OK. Tell yourself that you have an important job to do and to pull yourself together.

Tip 222: Visualise success	Essential

Visualisation can be a powerful tool for confidence and success.

Visualize yourself giving your speech. Imagine yourself speaking, your voice loud, clear and confident. Visualize your audience clapping. Visualise how you will reward yourself afterwards. Imagine how the load will be lifted off your shoulders when today is over.

Practice relaxation techniques before your presentation. Lie down or sit comfortably in a quiet place. Breathe slowly. Close your eyes. Scan your body, consciously relaxing any tense muscles. Imagine your upcoming speaking engagement. Picture yourself speaking with confidence. Make the details as sharp as possible, involving every sense.

- Concentrate on how good you are at public speaking.
- Pretend you are just chatting with a group of friends.
- Close your eyes and imagine your audience listening, laughing, and applauding.
- Remember happy moments from your past.
- Think about your love for and desire to help your audience.

Tip 223: Break out of the freeze	Advanced

"Freezing" is most people's biggest fear. You're standing before a room full of people and your mind goes blank. You can't remember a single thing you were planning on saying.

Many speakers freeze out of nerves. It can happen at the very beginning of you presentation or at any time during it, such as after you have been interrupted or distracted.

There are several tactics to help you recover from a freeze:

- While you're preparing your presentation make sure your main points flow logically from one to another. Make the connections really tight.

- Take a moment, take a breath, and think. If you give yourself half a chance you'll probably remember what you were going to say.

- Back up and try again. Repeat the previous point, the one you just summarized. Doing so will often lead you on to the next point.

- Refer to your notes.

- Don't focus on saying exactly the right words or memorising your speech. Focus, instead on communicating the concepts you have in mind.

- Tell your audience you've drawn a blank. Ask, "Where was I?" and someone will tell you.

- Say something. Say anything. The longer you stay silent -- trying to remember exactly what you had planned on saying -- the more stressed you will get.

Tip 224: You are going your audience a favour	Intermediate

Remember you are doing your audience a favour by sharing your data, information and take-home messages with them! Your message is important, interesting and relevant –it will be worthwhile for your audience to listen to your presentation.

Tip 225: Your audience wants you to succeed	Essential

Your audience has given up their time, effort and money to come and listen to what you have to say! They may even have paid to see your presentation. Nobody goes out and buys a car in the hope that it will break down!

Naturally your audience wants you to be interesting, stimulating, informative and entertaining. They want you to succeed. It would be a waste of their own time and energy if they did not pay attention to what you had to say. So they are not going to hate you or laugh at you. Your success is their success.

Tip 226: Use your built-in support group	Intermediate

By now you should have made friends with some people in the audience. If you are nervous, start your presentation by talking specifically to your new friends in the audience. Imagine you are having a conversation with them, rather than giving a speech. Just be yourself.

> See also:
>
> *"Tip 207: Meet your guests", page 117*

Tip 227: Have fun	Essential

Above all else, enjoy yourself and have fun. Smile as much as you can, and you will in turn feel happier and more positive about your presentation.

➢ Remember, no matter how nervous you are right now, you will feel great when you've finished!

Chapter 8: Delivering the presentation

*"In ancient times when Cicero had finished speaking,
the people said, 'How well he spoke,'
but when Demosthenes had finished speaking,
the people proclaimed, 'Let us march.'"*
– Adlai Ewing Stevenson II (1900-1965), American politician

Tip 228: Relax and smile!	Essential

When you are invited to the lectern to speak, take one long deep breath, stand up straight and walk over confidently.

When you reach the lectern and face your audience, the first thing you should do is relax and welcome them with a friendly smile. This is one important way to connect with your audience. A smile may be the single most powerful form of nonverbal communication.

Smiling and meeting your audience with a warm persona will put you in a better mood and mindset, and it will immediately have a positive effect on your audience – it will put them at ease too.

Imagine that you are meeting your best friend or spouse after a long time. Imagine how you would feel and react in that situation, and allow yourself to feel the same emotion at this moment.

Being up-tight, tense or over-formal at this point would be disastrous. It will create an unnecessary barrier between you and your guests. You are their leader for the duration of your presentation. When you are feeling relaxed and happy, they will feel relaxed and happy; when you are stressed and unhappy, they will also feel stressed and unhappy. You owe it to your audience to be totally engaged in the present... and smile.

Make eye contact with your audience and in particular, identify some friendly faces that you already know.

Standing straight and maintaining a healthy posture will make you look more comfortable and confident, and will help you voice sound richer.

Take at least one more deep breath and collect your thoughts. Pause for a moment, command their attention and then jump right into your presentation.

📖 *See also:*

"Tip 207: Meet your guests", page 117

Tip 229: Talk in the first and second person	Intermediate

To help build a better connection with your audience, speak in the first person (I, me, us, we) or second person (you), rather than in the third person (they, it).

Tip 230: Talk slower	Intermediate

It is a common mistake to talk too fast, especially when you are nervous or poorly prepared. This makes it a lot more difficult for your audience to understand what you are saying.

Tip 231: Be yourself	Intermediate

You want your audience to remember your presentation long after it is over. One of the ways you can make an impression is to stamp your own personality over your presentation. Your personality is the one thing about you that is unique and memorable! Let it come across in your presentation. Let your personality shine through. Why hide one of your biggest differentiators?

Be yourself, but remember that the presentation isn't about you – it's about your material. You're a conduit for relaying the information to your audience.

Everything that makes you unique – from your appearance to your beliefs, your experience, and your sense of humour – can be used in a way that wins you people's attention and respect.

Tip 232: Deliver confidently	Essential

You should aim to control your nerves for the duration of the presentation and present as confidently as possible.

Be unafraid. If you worry about making a fool of yourself or if you second guess your every word and gesture, you'll crush your natural enthusiasm and attractiveness.

Tip 233: Connect with your friends	Essential

You will already have made contact with people in the audience. Now when you stand up in front of your audience, make sure you use these newly found friends by talking to them during your presentation. Of course, don't talk to them at the exclusion of the rest of the audience, but it can be useful to start off by talking to them initially.

Tip 234: Refer to other speakers	Intermediate

You should aim to give a unique presentation each time. Your presentation should be tailored and personalised for each occasion that you deliver it. Each audience is a unique synthesis of different individuals, groups, locations, events, moods, themes and thoughts... it would be simplistic to deliver the same presentation every time.

Your presentation must acknowledge and reflect the uniqueness of the situation, otherwise there is little benefit of you being there – your audience may simply read your standard script at home.

You will achieve more interaction and get more satisfaction if you customise your talk for each audience. They will be able to relate and respond to your message better if you address their unique features.

A good way to customise the presentation is to mention speeches which have preceded yours or will come after yours. You may want to meet beforehand with other presenters who you know, or who are talking on the same subject matter and discuss the contents of your presentations so that each of you can cross-reference each others talks.

Tip 235: Be present in the moment	Advanced

Another good way to appear "in the moment" is to incorporate references to other things that your audience has experienced. Suppose you are at a conference and the lunch has been exceptionally good – reflect on that fact and share something in common with your unique audience that they could not have shared with you if they were not there that day.

Do not be occupied with thoughts of the future, of thoughts concerning what the results of your presentation might lead to. Do not ask about origins and ends leaving the moment forgotten. When you are with your audience, all that matters is that moment.

Tip 236: Don't air private grievance in public	Essential

You may not want to be there. Maybe someone pulled out at the last minute and asked you to cover? Don't share this with the audience.

If you are tired, unhappy, depressed, worried, or upset, your audience probably won't know it unless you draw attention to it.

Tip 237: Acknowledge the chairperson	Essential

If a chairperson is present, it is a courtesy to begin your presentation by thanking the chairperson for introducing you and inviting you to speak. The chairperson is also the person who will keep an eye on whether you are obeying your time allocation. It is the chairperson's responsibility to make sure you have all the facilities you need to perform at your best, so if there is anything you require, raise this with the chairperson.

Conversely, do not make the chairperson the focus of your talk. Do not refer to the chairperson constantly at the expense of the audience, or suck up to him/her. The chairperson is only a facilitator.

Tip 238: Move away from the lectern	Advanced

The podium and lectern have their place, and sometimes they are unavoidable. Lecterns can make a speaker look authoritative and in command. This is why politicians love speaking from behind a lectern. For most speakers, however, standing behind a lectern is like standing behind a wall; the last place you want to be is behind a wall.

➢ Do not stand behind the lectern.

Don't hide behind your papers on the lectern, and come out and meet your audience. The goal of your presentation is to connect with your audience. Removing physical barriers between you and your audience will help you build rapport and make a connection.

Tip 239: Move away from the podium	Advanced

Get closer to your audience by moving away from, or at least, in front of the podium.

Walk towards your audience. Walk in front of the screen, walk in the isles, walk down the sides, vary your standing position. This allows you to look directly at the majority of your audience, since most people sit in the back of the room.

Moving around the room allows you to maintain eye contact with every part of the audience. It gives the impression that each member of your audience is being addressed.

The most important time you need to see the screen is when you change slides. If you time it right, by walking back toward the front of the room you can see the entire slide without appearing as you needed to.

If you can't walk toward your audience, then at least lean in towards them. Move meaningfully with each point you make.

Tip 240: Make eye contact and smile	Essential

When you are delivering your presentation, be careful that you don't blankly stare at the back of the room or the floor. Also, do not just cast a general gaze around the room. Avoid the bad habit of randomly scanning around the room without looking at anything or anyone in particular.

➤ Do not stare at the lectern or your notes!

When you are nervous, you tend to talk 5 feet above your audience's heads. This is a quick way to disconnect from your audience.

To make a powerful connection with your audience you have to look people in the eye. What's a conversation without eye contact?

Your audience will connect with you if you talk to individual people rather than scanning the group. When you are talking you should be looking directly at someone in your audience as if you are engaging in a normal conversation with him or her. Talk to this person holding their gaze for a few seconds, then move on to someone else. Speak every word into the eyes and heart of each person.

Look into people's eyes with a soft gaze; don't force it or stare. And while you're maintaining great eye contact, don't forget to smile as well. Unless your topic is very grim, a smile can be a very powerful thing.

This eye contact is made harder if you have bright lights in your eyes, but you can usually still make out people in your audience, or at least imagine members of your audience being there.

Be careful not to ignore one side of the audience. Many speakers "side" unconsciously, looking always to the left or to the right half, or only to the front or the back of the room.

Tip 241: Do not look at the screen too much	Essential

A common mistake is to spend too much time looking at the screen. Why are you looking at the screen? You should be looking at your audience to make eye contact and get non-verbal cues and feedback!

It is acceptable to occasionally glance at the screen to make sure you are on the right slide or to use the slides for landmarking, but do not spend the entire presentation looking at your slides on the screen!

Tip 242: Talk – don't lecture	Intermediate

Talk like a human being. It's easier to understand, and it allows you to make genuine contact with your audience.

Further, it ultimately helps you to think more clearly, by forcing you to communicate your points in ordinary terms.

Tip 243: Use gestures	Intermediate

Be aware of nervous gestures which may be apparent in your body language. If you have ever videotaped yourself giving a presentation, you will soon pick up on these gestures.

Work to eliminate distracting or nervous gestures. Avoid excessive hands in pockets, clenched fists, pointing, hands on hips, hand under chin, folded arms around chest, and the infamous fig leaf position where your hands are crossed in front of your groin.

Do not spend too much time or energy to develop new gestures – they will come naturally, if you let them and encourage them.

Let your words trigger your actions. If you are counting, hold out your fingers. If you say no, shake your head no. If you are saying something nice, give a big smile. Hold your hands open and wide apart to show sincerity and honesty.

If you are giving a demonstration or intentionally gesticulating, bear in mind that the larger your audience, the larger, slower and more energetic your gestures will need to be. Conversely, if you have a small audience or if you are videoconferencing, use smaller gestures.

Tip 244: Take cues from your audience as you speak	Advanced

As you are giving your presentation, be attentive to non-verbal cues and feedback from your audience to determine if you are putting them to sleep or talking over their heads, for example.

Observe your audience for their reactions. You may be saying the right words in your presentation, but if you pay attention you'll realize that your audience is always communicating back to you.

➢ Listening while speaking takes practice.

Respond to what your audience is telling you. Shift gears. Don't be on autopilot. Deviate from your prepared material according to the needs and reactions of your audience.

If people seem to be falling asleep or getting restless or distracted, the problem may not be you. Is the room too hot or too cold? Is it too dark, or too noisy? Can people see you?

Is the microphone on? Is something outside the room distracting people? Don't hesitate to stop talking in order to solve these problems.

Alternatively, you may have gone on too long, or you may need to speak louder. Whatever the case, notice what's happening and use it as feedback. If you can't figure out why your audience is responding poorly, ask somebody later and fix the problem next time.

If you're not sure whether people can see or hear, ask someone in the back row directly. This is also a good technique for setting up initial communication with your audience. It makes listeners feel included, and puts you in touch with them as human beings.

Tip 245: Use a wireless pointer	Intermediate

To advance your slides, invest in a small, handheld wireless remote control pointer. It will allow you to move away from the podium. And give you the freedom to move around the room or podium stage as you like.

Tip 246: Avoid laser pointers	Intermediate

Your slides should be so clear that your audience can easily follow along without your using a laser pointer. If you must point to something, step up close to the screen and use your hand.

If you absolutely must use a pointer, put it down as soon as you have finished using it, otherwise you will use it for every point on every slide!

Tip 247: Use a microphone properly	Intermediate

If you are using a microphone, you will need to keep it the same distance from your mouth at all times. If you are a naturally loud speaker then this distance should be quite large. If you turn your head, the microphone must follow. Avoid getting near the loudspeakers because this will deafen everyone with feedback.

Tip 248: Explain the slide or prop as soon as you show it	Intermediate

As soon as you show your audience a slide or prop, they will look at it – even if you're talking about something else.

➢ Don't make them divide their attention between you and your slide or prop.

Only show the slide or prop when you are ready to use it and not a moment before.

Tip 249: Remove your slide when it has made its point	Advanced

As soon as your slide or prop has been used and is no longer required, remove it from your audience's field of attention. This will make sure that their attention naturally returns to you.

If you are not quite ready to move on to the next slide, simply make the screen go blank by pressing the "W" key to get a black white slide or the "B" key to get a blank black slide.

Then when you are ready to move on, simply press any key to return to your presentation.

📖 *See also:*

"Tip 120: Use blank slides", page 69

Tip 250: Ignore interruptions	Intermediate

In the course of your presentation you may experience some interruptions.

- People may enter or leave the room
- People may laugh at you unexpectedly
- People may start whispering to each other about something – you may think that they are talking about you

Don't be flustered or thrown off course. It is normal to have some interruptions during your presentation. Do your best despite the interruptions. The show must do on.

Try to regain your composure and your control on the situation. Speak a bit louder. Move around a bit. Become more animated. Talk a bit slower.

Above all else, don't get flustered or frustrated. Be patient and give the room time to refocus on you and your presentation.

Tip 251: Use a deeper voice	Intermediate

Psychologists will tell you that a deeper voice, and a voice that is richer and fuller is often perceived as being more credible than a weaker, high-pitched or inconsistently-pitched voice.

You can get a deeper voice by controlling your nerves, taking deep breaths, and breathing and speaking from the middle of your abdomen rather than from your throat.

Tip 252: Be prepared to stray from the script	Advanced

Don't be so fixated on your script or slides that you're afraid to stray a little.

Comments from your audience can help you get your point across better than anything you've prepared. You may also get an idea of their learning needs through a comment or question which can change the entire course of your presentation.

Be prepared to respond to this. Remember, you are there to meet the needs of your audience. Rigidly following the correct sequence of your slides is not the ultimate objective of your presentation. Giving your audience what they need is of paramount importance.

Tip 253: Give your audience something to think about	Advanced

Your audience can think at a rate of 600 words per minute. However, they can process your words at the very maximum rate of only 150 words a minute. This leave approximately 450 words a minute to think about lunch, friends, family, the weather or absolutely anything other than your presentation.

So, when you have said a few words, your audience has already raced ahead of you to something else. If those spare 450 words a minute find something to think about which is more interesting or pressing than your presentation, then the mind will naturally allocate more brainpower to think about the new interest, rather than thinking about your presentation!

There is no point speaking any faster, because your audience cannot understand your words any faster than 150 words a minute.

➤ To keep up with your audience, every 15 seconds or so, you must find something non-verbal to do in order to keep pulling your audience's focus back on to you.

This could be a movement around the stage, or changing a slide, or a gesture. Use your imagination to find something non-verbal approximately every 15 seconds which will keep your audience's eyes and thoughts entirely on you.

Tip 254: Watch the clock	Essential

It is almost inevitable that your delivery will not go at the same pace as when you had practiced it. Indeed, if your presentation is going slower than intended, this can be a good indicator that you have managed to be natural, that you have varied the tone and speed in response to live non-verbal feedback from your audience, or that there have been some spontaneous questions. All these are generally good things.

If your delivery is going faster than expected, then maybe you are being too nervous.

In both cases, the only way to know this is to keep an eye on the clock and relate that back to your time landmarks.

➤ Make sure you keep to your time allocation!

📖 *See also:*

"Tip 187: Make landmarks for timing", page 106

Tip 255: Don't let your throat dry out	Intermediate

Don't be shy about having a glass of water and taking drinks from it once or twice. Make sure however that you do it smoothly – don't let your audience see your hands shake from nerves!

Tip 256: If something goes wrong, laugh with it	Advanced

Things will go wrong from time to time, and audiences appreciate and are relaxed by presenters who can roll with it. Do not become so attached to your slides or props that you cannot put on a show without them. Your message is far greater than the technology helping you.

Tip 257: Plan for disaster	Essential

➤ Keep an eye on the nearest empty chair in case you start to feel faint...

Chapter 9: 'Any questions?'

"I have never met a man so ignorant that I couldn't learn something from him."
– Galileo Galilei (1564–1642), Italian physicist, astronomer and philosopher

Tip 258: Decide how to handle questions	Essential

In certain situations the chairperson will decide how the audience will ask any questions arising from your presentation. If you have any choice in this, take a moment to decide how you will handle questions.

You may want to invite your audience to interrupt and ask questions as and when they occur. The advantage of this is that your audience will feel free to interact with you, and your presentation will have a freer exchange of thoughts and opinions. The disadvantage of this strategy is that you and your audience may lose the flow of the presentation. Also, the questions that your audience asks may be answered later in your presentation.

An alternative technique for taking questions is to invite them all at the end. The advantage of this is that questions will not interrupt the flow of your presentation. Also, some questions which arise during your presentation will be naturally answered in the course of the presentation itself.

You may want to take questions directly from your audience, or ask them to write questions down and send them to the front.

In either case, make sure you give all members of your audience a chance to ask questions. If you cannot answer all the questions in the time available, make yourself available for question after the presentation, or provide your contact details so that people can write, phone or meet you at a later date.

Tip 259: Repeat the question if necessary	Intermediate

You must understand the question that is being asked. If you did not hear the question, do not hesitate to ask the questioner to repeat the question. If you do not understand the question, try asking the questioner for clarification or to re-phrase the question. You may want to rephrase the question yourself to check you have understood it correctly.

If someone asks a question in a large audience without using a microphone or if your presentation is being taped, you will need to repeat the question, possibly paraphrasing it for brevity.

Tip 260: Use questions to reinforce your main points	Intermediate

Answer questions as directly as possible without being abrupt. Correct factual errors or misunderstandings immediately. If you can best answer a question by explaining one of your slides, bring it back up. Don't simply repeat what you said the first time around. Use the slide to answer the specific question.

Use your answers to reinforce your main points, and avoid making a presentation about a whole new subject.

Begin your answer by addressing the questioner, and then widen out your attention to address the whole the audience.

Tip 261: Handle questions politely	Intermediate

Make sure you wait for the entire question to the asked before you start to reply. Always be courteous, gracious, tactful & professional in your dialogue with your audience.

Do thank the members of your audience for their questions and input, even if someone is being difficult. You must keep to the high ground, and at all times be a gentleman or lady and deal with such individuals courteously. The true professional can always remain cool and in control.

➢ Remember, it is your reputation, so always remain gracious even with the most challenging of audiences.

Never embarrass the questioner; always be respectful, and avoid sarcasm, criticism, or arrogance.

Finally: keep your sense of humour!

Tip 262: Tackle difficult questions	Advanced

Inevitably, you will sometimes be faced with questions that you cannot answer.

If a question is too complex or contentious to be answered in the time limit, then don't be afraid to say, "I don't know." Admit that there's more to be said, and ask for the person's business card and promise to get back to him or her with the answer.

Alternatively you may want to involve other presenters or turn certain questions back on your audience asking for their input as someone may be able to answer the question.

Example   "Wow – that's a great question, you must really understand quantum mechanics quite well. I'm not sure of the answer to that one, but I can definitely find out. Shall we discuss it straight after the presentation?"

Tip 263: Have your own questions ready	Intermediate

Some audiences will be slow to ask questions. To get them warmed up, you may want to begin with a question or two of your own.

> *Example*   "I often get asked how we can increase the yield of the TDPS sub-process in a low-pressure catalytic environment. That's a very good question because…"

Another way to seed the question & answer session is to leave a list a potential questions with a colleague, co-worker or friend in the audience. If no one else is forthcoming in asking questions, this person can start the ball rolling by asking your pre-prepared questions.

Tip 264: End the Q&A with a summary	Advanced

After you've answered the last question, wrap-up your presentation with a one or two sentence summary if you haven't already done so already. This can help to re-energize your audience and end your presentation with your take-home messages or action plan in the forefront of their attention.

Chapter 10: After the presentation

"You can make more friends in two months by becoming interested in other people than you can in two years of trying to get other people interested in you."
– Dale Carnegie (1888-1955), American writer

Tip 265: Hang about after the presentation	Essential

Try to be available after the presentation. Members of your audience may want to meet you to discuss your presentation. Place yourself near the exit doors at the end of your presentation so you can meet people, smile, shake hands, and make eye contact.

By doing so you may learn useful information or make contacts with potential clients, collaborators, patrons or employers.

Tip 266: Make contacts	Intermediate

Use the time after your presentation to exchange business cards and contact details with people – both members of the audience and other speakers alike – who share the same interests as you.

Always follow through any new contacts when you get home by making a phone call or sending an email.

Tip 267: Congratulate yourself	Essential

You did it! Your presentation is over and you can finally let your hair down and pat yourself on the back.

Tip 268: Get constructive feedback	Essential

If possible, get constructive feedback from someone you trust.

Tip 269: Learn from your experience	Essential

When you come back home and have mentally and physically recovered from your presentation, find the time to spend some quality time with yourself.

Write down some things that you did well in your presentation, and write down things that did not go well.

It is easy to think over what might have gone wrong during your presentation, but it is important to focus on positive aspects ensuring you repeat them next time, and think about the some aspects to improve on.

➢ Look through this book and see which tips you missed out on, and identify which tips or ideas you can implement in your next presentation.

Chapter 11: Final Thoughts

"When you are not practicing, remember, someone somewhere is practicing, and when you meet him he will win."
– Charles "Ed" Macauley (1928-), former American professional basketball player

I want to close this book by giving you some general advice about how you can improve your public speaking style and technique. I have intentionally left this section for the very end of the book, because compared with the tips in the earlier chapters many of the things I will say here cannot be actioned immediately but will require a longer-term approach to implement.

Presentation excellence is never accidental! Everyone needs to work hard at developing their skills.

It is a difficult process, but public speaking is so important that careers have been advanced or derailed based on a presentation. Deals have been won or lost depending on the outcome of a presentation. Non-profits and volunteer organizations have won funding or folded up their tents depending on their performance in a presentation.

Presentations matter. And it is something very worthy of our commitment and lifelong study.

Tip 270: Learn from good speakers and bad speakers alike	Essential

Stand back and learn from other speakers. You will have seen other speakers, both good and bad, and you should attempt to learn all you can from them. Perhaps the best way to become an excellent speaker yourself is to watch really good, experienced speakers and model your presentations on theirs.

Watch speakers who do it well and those who do it poorly. Analyse their content, their style, their delivery. What is it about those who do it well, that makes their presentations effective and memorable? And what is it about those who do it badly that makes them particularly memorable in a bad way?

Notice not just what they say, but what they do: how they move, how they use their voices, how they look at the audience, how they handle timing and questions.

Brainstorm the qualities of good speakers. When you find an excellent role model, work hard to emulate that person: you can't go wrong.

Compare your notes with what I have written in this book and make up your own mind of what works and what doesn't work. Decide for yourself what is useful and what is harmful.

If you do not have access to speakers and talks in the course of your workplace, consider attending public lectures at your local university, college, or other public institution. If you have broadband access to the internet, you can also try downloading video clips of successful speakers.

Tip 271: Practice public speaking	Intermediate

Seek out supportive audiences and go and speak at every opportunity. Speak in small forums where less is at stake, such as at staff meetings. Just get up in front of people over and over again, and keep doing it.

You might think that it takes confidence just to stand up and start talking. Be bold as a speaker, confident in your abilities. Practice every day, give speeches whenever you can.

Accept your mistakes as part of the learning process and accept constructive feedback.

Tip 272: Go on a course	Intermediate

Enrol yourself on a public speaking course where you can be taught the necessary skills and get plenty of opportunity to practice in a supportive and constructive environment.

Enquire at your local higher education institute, or search on the internet for suitable courses. You may be able to get your employer to subsidise the cost of such courses.

Tip 273: Join a club	Advanced

Toastmasters is an international association of speaking clubs. At Toastmasters, members learn by speaking to groups and working with others in a supportive environment. A typical Toastmasters club is made up of 20 to 30 people who meet once a week for about an hour.

Toastmasters clubs are an excellent way to improve your presentation and leadership skills.

➤ Local clubs can be found by visiting http://www.Toastmasters.org

Alternatively, consider engaging with voluntary organisations or local branches of service clubs such as Rotary or Lions Club. They often welcome offers from the public to speak on topics which may be of interest or benefit to their members.

Demosthenes

Demosthenes (384BC–322BC) was a prominent Greek statesman and orator of ancient Athens. His orations constitute the last significant expression of Athenian intellectual prowess and provide a thorough insight into the politics and culture of ancient Greece during the 4th century BC.

As a boy Demosthenes had suffered from a speech impediment, and an inarticulate and stammering pronunciation. According to Plutarch, he also had a weakness in his voice, "a perplexed and indistinct utterance and a shortness of breath, which, by breaking and disjointing his sentences much obscured the sense and meaning of what he spoke."

Demosthenes soon undertook a disciplined program to overcome these shortcomings and improve his locution. He worked on his diction, his voice and his gestures. Demosthenes used to study in an underground room he constructed himself. He also used to talk with pebbles in his mouth and recited verses while running. To strengthen his voice, he spoke on the seashore over the roar of the waves.

Demosthenes learned rhetoric by studying the speeches of previous great orators. He delivered his first judicial speeches at the age of twenty. He grew interested in politics during his time as a professional speech-writer and in 354 BC he gave his first public political speeches. He would go on to devote the most productive years of his life to opposing Macedon's expansion.

Bust of the Greek orator Demosthenes[1]

Demosthenes' language was simple and natural, never far-fetched or artificial. He was a true artist who could make his art obey him. The main criticism of Demosthenes' art, however, seems to have rested chiefly on his known reluctance to speak extempore; he often declined to comment on subjects he had not studied beforehand. However, he gave the most elaborate preparation to all his speeches and, therefore, his arguments were the products of careful study. He was also famous for his caustic wit.

According to Cicero, Demosthenes regarded "delivery" (gestures, voice etc.) as more important than style. He made efficient use of his body to accentuate his words. Thus he managed to project his ideas and arguments much more forcefully.

According to the classical scholar Harry Thurston Peck, Demosthenes "affects no learning; he aims at no elegance; he seeks no glaring ornaments; he rarely touches the heart with a soft or melting appeal, and when he does, it is only with an effect in which a third-rate speaker would have surpassed him. He had no wit, no humour, no vivacity, in our acceptance of these terms. The secret of his power is simple, for it lies essentially in the fact that his political principles were interwoven with his very spirit."

Demosthenes Practicing Oratory
by Jean Lecomte du Nouÿ [2]

The Alexandrian Canon compiled by Aristophanes of Byzantium and Aristarchus of Samothrace recognized Demosthenes as one of the 10 greatest Attic orators and speech-writers. According to Longinus, Demosthenes "perfected to the utmost the tone of lofty speech, living passions, copiousness, readiness, speed." Cicero acclaimed him as "the perfect orator" who lacked nothing, while Quintilian extolled him as "lex orandi" ("the standard of oratory") and underscored that "inter omnes unus excellat" ("he stands alone among all the orators").

Lightning Source UK Ltd.
Milton Keynes UK
UKOW07f1453100415

249436UK00004B/25/P

9 780955 487309